A Basic Course in
Modern Turkish

Peter Pikkert

ALEV
BOOKS

"Believe, Think, Act"

alevbooks.com

alevbooks@gmail.com

1ˢᵗ printing: 1999
2ⁿᵈ printing: 2010

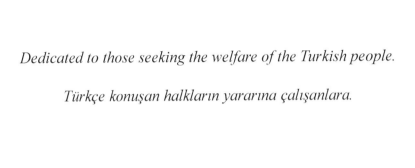

Dedicated to those seeking the welfare of the Turkish people.

Türkçe konuşan halkların yararına çalışanlara.

Contents

Preface

Welcome to the delightful world of Turkish, a world which combines near-mathematical precision with near-musical harmony.

This book seeks to provide a quick but comprehensive overview of the Turkish language. Its strength lies in its topical arrangement, its simple explanations and its index of suffixes for easy reference. In addition, the fact that every example is translated into English means that one is not left struggling with word meanings while trying to figure out a particular grammatical construction.

Although this book answers many questions about Turkish, the momentum of language learning is sustained through genuine friendships with nationals and not by burying oneself in books, cassettes and interactive DVDs. If this tool enables you to establish some meaningful relationships with Turks, you have made me a happy man.

I want to thank Aylin Aykın, İsa Karataş, Hakan Çevikoğlu and Mike O'Donnell for their invaluable critiques of the manuscript. Any shortcomings this book has are my fault, not theirs.

Peter Pikkert

Chapter 1

The Alphabet, Vowel Harmony, the Indefinite Article, Personal Pronouns and Plurals

1.1 - The Alphabet

The Turkish alphabet has eight vowels and twenty-one consonants. The vowels are approximately as follows:

a - as in "car" and "bar".
e - as in "met" and "led".
ı - as in "cousin", "caution" and "motion".
i - as in "sea" and "lee".
o - as in "cone" and "load" (but with no offglide: [o] not [ou]).
    When lengthened as in "<u>awe</u>some".
ö - as in the German "Köln" or the French "peur".
u - as in "boot" or "who".
ü - as in the German "Führer" or the French "tu".

The consonants are approximately as follows:

b - as in "boy".
c - as in "John" and "joke".
ç - as in "chunk" and "peach".
d - as in "dog".
f - as in "fire" but with less emphasis than in English.
g - as in "girl".
ğ - lengthens the previous vowel, though is sometimes pronounced as
    a light "y" or "w". It doesn't occur at the beginning of words.
h - as in "house".

j - as in "measure" and "seizure".
k - as in "car" and "kilo".
l - as in "lad" and "leave".
m - as in "man"
n - as in "man".
p - as in "peg".
r - as in "ribbon".
s - as in "sad".
ş - as in "shut" and "hush".
t - as in "toy" and "take".
v - as in "voice". It is pronounced slightly lighter than in English.
y - as in "yes".
z - as in "zoo".

A few, often foreign, words that end in voiced consonants such as "b", "c", "d", and "g" change their last consonant to "p", "ç", "t", and "k" respectively when standing alone.

When the word becomes part of a compound noun or when suffixes are added to it the word reverts to its original form: "kitab" ("book" in original Arabic form) > "kitap" (in Turkish) > "kitabevi" (bookstore).

Turkish is written the way it is spoken. With the exception of "ğ", there are no silent letters. By accidentally deleting a letter you run the risk of changing the meaning of a word.

1.2 - Vowel Harmony

Turkish is based on adding suffixes to root words. Although the consonants in the suffixes are, by and large, stable, the suffixes' vowels tend to adapt to the last vowel in the root word. This is called vowel harmony.

In general
"a" causes the suffix vowels to change to "a" or "ı"
"e" causes the suffix vowels to change to "e" or "i"
"i" causes the suffix vowels to change to "i" or "e"
"o" causes the suffix vowels to change to "a" or "u"
"ö" causes the suffix vowels to change to "ü" or "e"
"u" causes the suffix vowels to change to "u" or "a"
"ü" causes the suffix vowels to change to "ü" or "e"
"ı" causes the suffix vowels to change to "ı" or "a"

Foreign words (often Arabic, Persian or French imports) tend to break vowel harmony.

In this book we will not repeat all the forms of the suffixes each time but expect the reader to realize that most suffixes come in one of four forms. For instance, "-im" (my) can also be "-üm", "-ım", or "-um".

ceket-im - my jacket
göz-üm - my eye
kitab-ım - my book
tuz-um - my salt

Note: We will insert a dash (-) before newly introduced suffixes. Suffixes covered in preceding chapters will not be preceded by a dash.

1.3 - Gender and the Indefinite Article.

Turkish has no such thing as gender, nor is there a definite article (i.e the word "the"). The word "bir" (one) is used as the indefinite article "a" or "an", but can also mean "some", "something", "only", "once", and "just a bit". Nouns qualified by "bir" are not, however, necessarily indefinite. The accusative case, as we will see later, often indicates definiteness.

Bir adam - A man
Bir adamı - a particular man ("-ı" is the accusative case ending, which will be covered later).
Bir şey yok - There is nothing.
Bir Allah bilir - Only God knows.
Bir bu kaldı - Only this remains.

1.4 - The Personal Pronouns

ben - I	biz - we
sen - you	siz - you (pl.)
o - he/she/it	onlar - they

1.5 - The Possessive Suffixes

After consonants	*After vowels*	*English equivalents*
- im	- m	my
- in	- n	your (singular)
- i	- si	his/her/its
- imiz	- miz	our
- iniz	- niz	your (plural)
- leri/ları	- leri/ları	their

defter-im - my notebook   defter-imiz - our notebook
defter-in - your notebook   defter-iniz - your (pl.) notebook
defter-i - his notebook   defter-leri - their notebook

araba-m - my car   araba-mız - our car
araba-n - your car   araba-nız - your (pl.) car
araba-sı - his car   araba-ları - their car

kitab-ım - my book
göz-ü - his eye
masa-nız - your (pl.) table.

An "-n-" buffer is inserted after the third person if other suffixes follow.

göz-ü-n-e - to her eye ("-e" means "to" or "for", see 3.5)

The sole exception is "su" (water), which uses a "-y-" buffer.

su-y-u - its water (see. 3.3)
su-y-unuz - your (pl.) water

1.6 - Uses of the Third Person Singular Suffix

The Turkish suffix "-(s)i" is very important.

a. It can be used as the third person singular ending (see 1.5).

b. It can relate the word to which it is attached to a previous word.

Alman hükümet-i - The German government
Türkiye Cumhuriyet-i - The Turkish Republic

c. It can relate the word to which it is attached to a word in the genitive case (see 3.4).

d. It can relate the word to which it is attached to a word (often a pronoun) which is understood from the context (see 3.4).

e. It can be used to form compound nouns. Compound nouns don't follow vowel harmony in their internal structure. Note, too that not all compound nouns use the third-person suffix.

denizaltı - submarine (deniz + alt + ı)
hanımeli - honeysuckle (hanım + el + i) kızkardeş -
sister (kız + kardeş)
anayasa - constitution (ana + yasa)
başkent - capital city (baş + kent)

1.7 - Plurals

Plurals are formed by adding either the suffix "-ler" or "-lar" (depending on vowel harmony). It precedes any other suffixes which might be tagged on as well. The plural suffixes occur only in the "-ler" and "-lar" forms.

mektup - letter > mektup-lar - letters
gazete - newspaper > gazete-ler - newspapers
adamlar - men
gözler - eyes
kıtaplar - books
ceketler - jackets

Plurals are not used when denoting class.

Çok mektup - Many letters
Çok gazete - Many newspapers

1.8 - "Var" and "Yok"

"Var" (having/existing) and "yok" (non-existent) are sometimes used when one would use "yes" (evet) or "no" (hayır) in English.

Yer var mı? - Is there a place? ("mı" is an interogative particle; see 8.5)
Evet, var. - Yes there is.
Gazete var mı? - Are there any newspapers?
Yok - No.

1.9 - Modes of address

abla - older sister (used informally with women slightly older than oneself)
ağabey (or simply "abi") - older brother (used informally with men slightly older than oneself)
amca - uncle

bay (B.) - Mr.

bayan (Bn.) - Mrs, Miss.

beyefendi - polite term for men

efendi - used after the given names of male servants. "Hasan efendi."

efendim - used to address anyone. Is also used as "I beg your pardon?" and as a "stop word" used in the middle of a sentence to give one time to think.

hanım - used to address a lady.

hanımefendi - polite term for women.

sayın (Sn.) - used to address men on formal occasions.

paşa - used to address generals and ambassadors.

usta - used to address skilled tradesmen.

Endless terms used for various personal relationships are also used to address any stranger. There are also numerous terms of endearment.

Note: "karıkoca" means "wife and husband" while "kocakarı" means "old hag"!

1.10 - Common Expressions

Affedersiniz - Excuse me

Afiyet olsun - Bon appetit

Allahaısmarladık - Goodbye (said by person leaving to person staying)

Allah rahatlık versin - "May God give ease" (i.e, good night)

Alo - Hello (used when answering the phone)

Bana müsaade - If you'll excuse me (said when wanting to leave)

Baş üstüne - On my head (it shall be done)

Çok şükür - Many thanks (in response to "nasılsınız")

Estağfurullah - said when someone flatters you or when someone else belittles him/herself

Gözünüz aydın - Congratulations (said when one has waited long for something good to happened)

Güle güle - Goodbye (said by person staying to person leaving)

Güle güle kullanın - use laughingly (said to someone who has just bought some non-consumable object)

Günaydın - Good morning

Hamdolsun - Let there be praise! (Possible response to "nasılsınız?"

Hoş bulduk - response to "hoş geldiniz" (welcome)

Hoşça kalın - stay well (informal)

İyi akşamlar - Good evening

İyi geceler - Good nigh

İyi günler - Good day

İyi yolculuklar - Have a good journey

İyilik sağlık - Goodness and health (possible response to "ne var ne yok")

Maşallah - Said when admiring someone else's baby. (Don't express outright admiration as that is considered inviting bad luck.)

Kolay gelsin - May it come easy (said when encountering people who are working)

Kusura bakmayın - Don't look at my fault (i.e. Excuse me)

Memnun oldum - said when introduced to someone new

Merhaba - Hello

Nasılsınız? - How are you?

Ne var ne yok? - How are things? (informal)

Sıhhatler olsun - Let there be health (said to someone who has just had a bath, a shave or a haircut). Note that vowel harmony is broken because "sıhhat" is an Arabic word.

Size de - To you as well (convenient response to many greetings and blessings)

Teşekkür ederim, iyiyim - Thank you, I'm fine.

Ziyade olsun - said when others are eating but you don't want to.

Atasözü - Proverb

Bir inat bir murat

A stubbornness a goal
(A determined man will reach his goal)

Chapter 2

Verbs

2.1 - The Verb "to be" in the Present Tense

The present tense of the verb "to be" is not formed by an independent word but with the suffixes "-im", "-sin", "-iz", "-siniz", "-dirler" (or their mutations according to the rules of vowel harmony). In the third person the ending is optional. Also note that it is not necessary to use the personal pronouns (see 1.4), since the ending communicates who is referred to. The pronouns are only used for emphasis.

İngiliz-im - I am English   İngiliz-iz - we are English
İngiliz-sin - you are English   İngiliz-siniz - you are English
İngiliz(-dir) - he/she/it is English   İngiliz(-dirler) - they are English

Türk-üm - I am (a) Turk   Türk-üz - we are Turks
Türk-sün - you are (a) Turk   Türk-sünüz - you (pl.) are Turks
Türk-tür - he/she/it is (a) Turk   Türk(türler) - they are Turks

After words ending in a vowel a "y" is added as a buffer between the word and the suffix.

Amerikalı-y-ım - I am American
İstanbullu-y-uz - We are (from) Istanbul

2.2 - The Verb "to be" in the Negative

The negative of "to be" (i.e. not to be) is expressed using the word "değil" (not), with the appropriate suffixes of the verb "to be".

değil-im - I am not   değil-iz - we are not
değil-sin - you are not   değil-siniz - you (pl.) are not
değil(-dir) - he/she/it is not   değil(-dirler) - they are not

18

Hasta değil-im - I am not sick.
Güzel değil(-dir) - He/she/it is not nice.
Beyaz değil, siyah - He/she/it is not white, (but) black.
Türk değil-siniz - You (pl.) are not Turks.
Öğretmen değil-sin - You (sing.) are not (a) teacher.
Amerikalı değil-dirler - They are not American.
Boş değil - It is not empty.
Hoş değil - It is not pleasant.

2.3 - The Infinitive and the Verb Stem

The infinitive consists of the verb stem plus the suffix "-mek" or "-mak".
Dictionaries list verbs in their infinitive form. The verb stem is formed by
dropping the "-mek" or "-mak" suffix.

Git-mek (to go) > git (verb stem of "gitmek")
al-mak (to take) > al (verb stem of "almak")

Different suffixes are added to the verb stems to indicate person, tense, etc.
The verb stems are also the imperative forms of the verb.

Git! - Go!   Al! - Take!

2.4 - The Past Tense

As noted above, verb tense is formed by adding certain suffixes to the verb
stem. The past tense suffix is "-di".

Ver-mek (to give) > ver- (verb root of "vermek")
ver-dim - I gave	ver-dik - we gave
ver-din - you gave	ver-diniz - you (pl.) gave
ver-di - he/she/it gave	ver-diler - they gave

Bir kitap ver-dim - I gave a book.
Ders ver-di - He gave a lesson.
Para ver-diler - They gave money.
Ekmek ver-dik - We gave bread.

ol-mak (to be, to become) > ol
ol-dum - I became	ol-duk - we became
ol-dun - you became	ol-dunuz you (pl.) became
ol-du - he/she/it became	ol-dular - they became

Hasta ol-duk - We became sick.
Öğretmen ol-du - He became a teacher.
Amerikalı ol-dum - I became an American.
Türk ol-dular - They became Turks.

Yap-mak (to do, to make) > yap
yap-tım - I did/made   yaptık - we did/made
yap-tın - you did/made   yap-tınız - you (pl.) did/made
yap-tı - he/she/it made   yap-tılar - they did/made

Bir ev yap-tım - I made a house.
Ders yap-tılar - They did (their) lesson.
Çay ya-ptık - We made tea.
Ne yap-tınız? - What did you do?

2.5 - The Verb "to be" in the Past Tense

It will be remembered that the verb "to be" is understood in the present tense. In the past tense however, it is formed as follows.

idim - I was   idik - we were
idin - you were   idiniz - you (pl.) all were
idi - he/she/it was   idiler - they were

Hasta idim - I was sick.
Kapıcı idin - You were a doorman.
Öğretmen idi - He was a teacher.
Orada idik - We were there.

You can also connect these endings to the words they modify. Note that the "i" turns into a "y" following a vowel and is dropped altogether following a consonant. They then become subject to vowel harmony.

Hasta-y-dım -I was sick.
Kapıcı-y-dın - You were a doorman.
Öğretmen-di - He was a teacher.
Orada-y-dık - We were there.

2.6. - The Present Tense Suffix "-yor".

The present tense suffix is "yor" preceded by a vowel, according to the rules of vowel harmony.

gelmek (to come) > gel-i-yor (he/she/it is coming) i.e, gel (verb stem) + "i" (vowel) + "yor" (present tense suffix) = geliyor (he is coming).

gör-mek (to see) > gör-ü-yor (he is seeing)
al-mak (to take) > al-ı-yor (he is taking)
bul-mak (to find) > bul-u-yor (he is finding)
ol-mak (to become) > ol-u-yor (he is becoming)

Generally when the verb stem already ends in a vowel, the "-yor" suffix is added directly onto the stem.

taşı-mak (to carry) > taşı-yor (he is carrying)
koru-mak (to protect) > koru-yor (he is protecting)

Sometimes the "-yor" suffix changes the stem's vowel.

de-mek (to say) > di-yor (he is saying)
söyle-mek (to tell) > soylü-yor (he is telling)
anla-mak (to understand) > anlı-yor (he understands)

2.7 - Present Tense Suffix "-yor" and the Personal Endings

gel-i-yor-um - I am coming   gel-i-yor-uz - we are coming
gel-i-yor-sun - you are coming   gel-i-yor-sunuz - you (pl.) are coming
gel-i-yor - he/she/it is coming   gel-i-yor-lar - they are coming

yap-ı-yor-um - I am doing   yap-ı-yor-uz - we are doing
yap-ı-yor-sun - you are doing   yap-ı-yor-sunuz - you (pl.) are doing
yap-ı-yor - he/she/it is doing   yap-ı-yor-lar - they are doing

Note: the "-dir" third person singular ending is generally not added to "-yor".

2.8 - The Past Continuous Tense

By attaching the past tense suffixes to the present tense "-yor" suffix you form the past continuous tense. Note that the verb root is "git" (git-mek). The "t" changes to a "d" in this instance.

gid-i-yor-du-m - I was going   gid-i-yor-du-k - we were going
gid-i-yor-du-n - you were going   gid-i-yor-du-nuz – you (pl.) were
                                                                        going
gid-i-yor-du - he/she/it was going   gid-i-yor-du-lar – they were going

2.9 - Compound Verbs

A number of verbs are formed with the helping verb "etmek" (to do).

> yardım etmek - to help (i.e., yardım ediyorum - I am helping, etc.)
> teşekkür etmek - to thank (teşekkür ediyorum, etc.)
> kabul etmek - to accept
> telefon etmek - to phone

Sometimes the helping verb "etmek" is attached to the word it modifies:

> af (pardon) >affetmek (to pardon)
> sabır (patience) > sabretmek (to show patience)

The verbs "eylemek" and "kılmak" were once common as well, but they are rare today. However, "eylemek" is still used regularly in the expression "Allah rahmet/merhamet eylesin" (may God have mercy on him/her) and "kılmak" is still used with the expression "namaz kılmak" (to go through the rites of Muslim prayer).

2.10 - Transitive Verbs Without a Direct Object

When the direct object of a verb which is normally transitive is left off, Turkish tends to provide an object based on the root concept of the verb.

> Ablam yazı yaz-ıyor - My older sister is writing (a writing).
> Yemek yi-yoruz - We are eating (food).
> Kızım dikiş dik-iyor - My girl (daughter) is sewing (stitches).
> Komşumuz çok içki iç-iyor - Our neighbour drinks a lot (of alcohol).

Normally, however, transitive verbs are preceded by their objects, which take one of six cases, cases which are often used where we would use a preposition in English. It is all explained in the next chapter.

Atasözü - Proverb

Beş parmağın beşi bir değil.

The five fingers are not all one

(People are all different)

Chapter 3

Case

3.1 - Case

In English the case of a noun or pronoun shows its grammatical relationship to the rest of the sentence (i.e. whether it is acting or being acted upon, etc.). In Turkish, however, this is not necessarily so. Nevertheless case endings are very important in Turkish because they are used where we would use prepositions in English.

Turkish has six cases: the nominative, the accusative, the genitive, the dative, the locative and the ablative.

3.2 - The Nominative Case (or "Absolute Form")

The nominative case is simply the word as it stands without any case endings. It is how you will find it in the dictionary. This doesn't mean that words in the nominative case are necessarily the subject of the sentence. They can also be the object of the sentence, which is why some grammarians prefer calling this the "absolute form". In the examples below the words "adam" (man) and "çay" (tea) are the subject of the sentence in the first example and the object of the verb in the second example.

> Adam geliyor - (A) man is coming.
> Bir adam görüyorum - I see a man.
> Çay yok - There is no tea.
> Çay aldık - We bought tea.

3.3 - The Accusative (or Definite Objective) Case

The accusative case is used when a word is the object of a verb. However, it also makes that object definite (i.e where in English we would use the word "the"). That is why some grammarians refer to it as the "definite objective case". It is formed by adding the suffix "-i" (or "-ı", "-ü", or "-u", according to vowel harmony) to the word.

> Adam-ı gördüm - I saw the man.
> Süt-ü içti - He drank the milk.
> Gazete-y-i okuduk - We read the newspaper (the "-y-" is a buffer between the last vowel in the word and the suffix vowel.)
> Lahmacun-u yedin - You ate the lahmacun. (Lahmacun is a type of small, light pizza)
> Köpeğ-i gördüler - They saw the dog. (When a word ends in a "k", as in "köpek", the "k" changes to a "ğ" before case endings beginning with a vowel.)

3.4 - The Genitive (or Possessive) Case

The genitive (or possessive) case is used where English would use the word "of" or "-'s" to denote possession. It is formed b adding the suffix "-in" to the possessor and the suffix "-i/-ı/-u/-ü" to the object which he/she/it possesses.

> Adam-ın kalem-i - The man's pen.
> Öğretmen-in kitab-ı - The teacher's book.
> Yol-un kenar-ı - The side of the road.
> Gün-ün iş-i - The day's work.

Words in the genitive are generally understood to be in the definite (i.e. in the English translations we'd include the word "the"). Also, when a word ends in a vowel the genitive uses an "-n-" as a buffer for the possessor and a "-s-" as a buffer for the thing possesed.

> Kedi-n-in süt-ü - The cat's milk.
> Mustafa-nın arkadaş-ı - Mustafa's friend.
> Doktor-un oda-s-ı - The doctor's room.
> Adam-ın çanta-s-ı - The man's briefcase.
> Kız-ın güzel gözler-i - The girl's pretty eyes.
> Bu ev-in bir pencere-s-i - One window of this house.
> Amcam-ın bir ineğ-i - One of my uncle's cows.

The genitive case endings can be attached to words (often pronouns and/or adjectives) which are understood from the context.

> Bu-n-un daha güzel-i var - There is nicer (stuff) than this.

3.5 - The Dative Case

The dative case shows who or what the recipient or destination of a particular action is. As such it tends to be used with verbs of motion. The dative case is used where English would use the prepositions "to" or "for" or, in some instances, "at", "into", "on" and, rarely "after". It is formed by adding the suffix "-e" or "-a" (depending on vowel harmony) to the object of the appropriate verb.

Ev-e gidiyorum - I am going home.
Kız-a bakıyorum - I am looking at the girl.
Araba-y-a gidiyor - He is going to the car ("-y-" is a buffer).
Adam-a söyledim - I told (to) the man.
İstanbul'a vardılar - They arrived in Istanbul (an "-'-" separates
   proper nouns from case endings).

Tablo-y-a bakıyor - He/she is looking at the painting.
Çiçekler-i o-n-a getirdim - I brought the flowers for her ("-i" is the
   accusitive case ending, "-n-" is a buffer, "-a" is the dative case
   ending).
Çorba-y-a kara biber koydu - She put black pepper in the soup.
Yerim-e oturdu - He sat in my place.

The dative is also used with a number of words which correspond to English prepositions.

-e/-a doğru - towards
-e/-a göre - according to, suitable for, in view of
-e/-a kadar, -e/-a dek - as far as, until (also translates as "in", in this
   sense: "he will come in ten minutes" (On dakika-y-a kadar
   gelecek)
-e/-a ait - concerning, pertaining to, belonging to
-e/-a karşı - against, facing
-e/-a rağmen - in spite of

Ev-e doğru yürüdü - He walked toward the house.
Bana göre bu doğru değil - In my opinion this is not right.
Ev-e kadar yürüdü - He walked as far as the house.
Okul-a ait malzemeler - The things which pertain to school.
Hükümet-e karşı direnenler - Those who are against the government.
Her şey-e rağmen seni seviyorum - I love you in spite of everything.

3.6 - The Locative Case

The locative case is used where English would use the preposition "in", "on", or, in some cases, "at". It is formed by adding the suffixes "-de", "-da", "-te", or "-ta", depending on vowel harmony and whether or not the word ends in an unvoiced consonant.

> Ev-de - In the house
> Okul-da - At school
> Otobüs-te - In the bus
> İstanbul-da (after proper nouns written as İstanbul'da) - In Istanbul
> Maç-ta - At the match

The locative case is also used with words denoting a certain quality.

> Şarap rengin-de bir araba - A wine-coloured car.
> Kaş yaşın-da? - How old (is he/she/it)?
> Sekiz metre uzunluğun-da bir ip - An eight meter long rope.

3.7 - The Ablative Case

The ablative case indicates the point of origin or departure and is used where English would use the prepositions "from", "out", "of, "through", or "than". It is formed by adding the suffixes "-den", "-dan", "-ten" or "-tan".

> Ev-den geldik - We came from home (house).
> Kapı-dan geçti - He passed through the door.
> Maç-tan geldiler - They came from the match. Dükkan-dan
> çıktım - I left (from) the store.
> İzmit-ten (İzmit'ten) geldin - You came from Izmit.
> Çocuklar-dan biri - One of the children.
> On-dan haberim yok - I have no news of him
> Bura-dan geçmediler - They didn't pass through here.

The ablative is often used in comparisons (see 6.2). It is also used to show what something is made of.

> Ayşe-y-e kağıt-tan bir şapka yaptım - I made a hat from paper for Ayşe.
> Şu ev ahşap-tan yapıldı - That house was made of wood.

3.8 - Qualifying Nouns

The "-i" ending used in the accusative case can, in some cases, also be used by itself to mark words that are in a close relationship to each other (in English we either make a compound word or separate the two words which modify each other with a hyphen).

sinema (cinema) + bilet (ticket) > sinema bilet-i (cinema ticket)
el (hand) + çanta (bag) > el çanta-s-ı (handbag)
keçi (goat) + deri (skin) > keçi deri-s-i (goat skin/leather)
çay (tea) + bardak (glass) > çay bardağ-ı (tea glass)
1959 + yıl (year) > 1959 yıl-ı (the year of 1959)
misafir (guest) + oda (room) > misafir oda-s-ı (guest room)

3.9 - Personal Pronouns with Case Endings

nom.	ben - I	sen - you	o - he/she/it
acc.	beni - me	seni - you	onu - him/her/it
gen.	benim - mine	senin - your	onun - his/hers/its
dat.	bana - to/for me	sana - to/for you	ona - to/for him/her/ it
loc.	bende - in me	sende - in you	onda - in him/her/it
abl.	benden - from me	senden - from you	ondan - from him/her/it

nom.	biz - we	siz - you (pl.)	onlar - they
acc.	bizi - us	sizi - you	onları - they
gen.	bizim - our	sizin - your	onların - their
dat.	bize - to/for us	size - to/for you	onlara - to/for them
loc.	bizde - in us	sizde - in you	onlarda - in them
abl.	bizden - from us	sizden - from you	onlardan - from them

3.10 - The Demonstratives

bu - this (right here)
şu - this/that (over there)
o - that (way over there)

As in English, the demonstratives can be used as either adjectives or as pronouns.

O kadın - That woman.
O farklı - He/she/it is different
Bu radyo bozuk - This radio is broken.
Bu-n-u kim yaptı? - Who did this?

Şu çocuklar - Those children.

Derivatives from from "bu", "şu" and "o" are:

böyle - this, in this way, like this, such
şöyle - thus, in this/that way, like this/that, such
öyle - this, in that way, like that, such-and-such

Böyle konuştu - He spoke this way.
Şöyle baktı - He looked (gazed) like this.
Öyle yakışıklı bir adam - Such a handsome man.

3.11 - Postpositions With Absolute or Genitive Case

The singular pronouns ("ben", "sen", "o", "biz", "bu", "şu" and "kim" - who), but not the plurals ("onlar", "bizler" etc.), take the genitive suffix before the following postpositions: "ile" (with, by means of), "gibi" (like),"kadar" (as ... as) and "için" (for/in order to).

benim ile - with me
bunun gibi - like this
onun kadar çirkin - as ugly as he/she/it
sizin için - for you

Other words remain in the absolute form.

anneniz ile - with your mother
turp gibi - like a radish (expression used to describe good health)
Hülya kadar güzel - as beautiful as Hülya
sizler için - for you

"ile" undergoes a change similar to "idi" when suffixed, as it usually is. After a consonant it loses its- "i". Note that "-le" is changed to "la" with back vowels.

Benim ile > benimle - with me
at ile > atla - with a horse / by horse

After a vowel the "i" becomes "y".

araba ile > araba-yla - with (by) car
babası ile > babası-yla - with her/his father
annesi ile > annesi-yle - with her/his mother

"ile" may be reinforced with "birlikte" or "beraber" (together).

Öğrenciler-le birlikte Istanbul'u gezdi - Together with the students he went round Istanbul.
Komşumuz-la beraber sinemaya gittik - We went to the cinema   with our neighbours.

Atasözü - Proverb

Cahilden kork, aslandan korkma.

Fear a fool, don't fear a lion.

Chapter 4

The Future and Aorist Tenses, Forming the Negative

4.1 - The Future Tense

The future tense is formed by adding "-ecek/-acak" plus a personal ending to the verb stems. The "k" becomes a "ğ" when followed by a vowel.

gid-eceğim - I shall go
gid-eceksin - you will go
gid-ecek - he/she/it will go
gid-eceğiz - we shall go
gid-eceksiniz - you will go
gid-ecekler - they will go

Yarın okula gideceğim - Tomorrow I will go to school.
Yarın İstanbul'a gid-ecekler - Tomorrow they will go to İstanbul
Öğleden sonra buraya gel-ecek - He will come here in the afternoon.

4.2 - The Future Past Tense

The future past tense is formed by adding the past tense ending to the future tense suffix.
gid-ecek-tim - I was going to go
gid-ecek-tin - you were going to go
gid-ecek-ti - he/she/it was going to go
gid-ecek-tik - we were going to go
gid-ecek-tiniz - you were going to go
gid-ecek-lerdi or gid-ecek-tiler - they were going to go

Yarın kiliseye gid-ecek-tim - I was going to go to church tomorrow.
Haftaya Ankara'ya gid-ecek-tiniz - You were going to go to Ankara next week.

4.3 - The Aorist Tense

The aorist (or "unbounded") tense expresses the idea of habitually or regularly doing something, a readiness or willingness to do something, or an ability to do something.

To form the aorist tense an "-r" is added to verb stems which end in a vowel while those which end in a consonant receive an "-er", "-ar", "-ır", "-ir", "-ür", or "-ur" depending on vowel harmony.

Take, for example, the verb "yazmak" (to write). "Yazıyorum" (the regular present tense) means "I am writing right now". In the aorist tense "yazarım" means either "I write regularly", "I can write but am not doing so at the moment", or "I am prepared to write (it)".

almak (to take) > al-ır (he takes)
anla-mak (to understand) > anla-r (he understands)
bil-mek (to know) > bil-ir (he knows)
bul-mak (to find) > bul-ur (he finds)
çık-mak (to go out/up) > çık-ar (he goes out/up)
de-mek (to say) > de-r (he says)
et-mek (to do) > ed-er (he does).   the "t" changes to a "d".
gel-mek (to come) > gel-ir (he comes)
git-mek (to go) > gid-er (he goes) Note that the "t" changes to a "d"
gör-mek (to see) > gör-ür (he sees)
sor-mak (to ask) > sor-ar (he asks)
taşı-mak (to carry) > taşı-r (he carries)

4.4 - The Aorist Tense and the Present Tense Personal Endings

gör-ür-üm - I see   söyle-r-im -1 tell
gör-ür-sün - you see   söyle-r-sin - you tell
gör-ür - he/she/it sees   söyle-r - he/she/it tells
gör-ür-üz - we see   söyle-r-iz - we tell
gör-ür-sünüz - you (pl.) see   söyle-r-siniz - you (pl.) tell
gör-ür-ler - they see   söyle-r-ler - they tell

4.5 - The Aorist Tense and the Past Tense Personal Endings

gör-ür-düm -1 used to see   yap-ar-dım - I used to do
gör-ür-dün - you used to see   yap-ar-dın - you used to do
gör-ür-dü - he/she/it used to see yap-ar-dı - he/she/it used to do

gör-ür-dük - we used to see   yap-ar-dık - we used to do
gör-ür-dü-nüz - you used to see yap-ar-dınız - you used to do
gör-ür-lerdi - they used to see yap-ar-lardı - they used to do

4.6 - Other Uses of the Aorist Tense

a. The aorist tense is often used in polite requests (see 8.5).

b. The aorist tense is also often used in promises.

> Giderim - I'll go.
> Yaparım - I'll do (it).
> Veririm - I will give (it).

c. The aorist tense is used in a number of useful expressions and in many proverbs.

> Teşekkür ederim - thank you.
> Affedersiniz - I beg your pardon, excuse me.
> Olur - it happens, it is possible, it is alright, it is O.K.
> Olmaz (negative aorist, see 4.10) - it does not happen, it won't do, no way.
>
> İt ürür, kervan yürür - The dog howls, the caravan goes on ("ürür" is aorist of "ürümek" - to howl).

4.7 - Forming the Negative

The negative suffix is "-me" or "-ma". It is subject to vowel harmony only in the present tenses (i.e., those using the suffix "-yor"). The negative suffix is added right after the vowel root. The syllable just before the negative suffix is heavily accented.

> almak (to take) > al-ma-mak (not to take)
> gelmek (to come) > gel-me-mek (not to come)
> görmek (to see) > gör-me-mek (not to see)
> olmak (to be/become) > ol-ma-mak (not to be/not to happen)
> yapmak (to do, to make) > yap-ma-mak (not to do/not to make)

4.8 - The Negative with the Present Tense Personal Endings

gel-mi-yorum - I am not coming
gel-mi-yorsun - you are not coming
gel-mi-yor - he/she/it is not coming
gel-mi-yoruz - we are not coming
gel-mi-yorsunuz - you (pl.) are not coming
gel-mi-yorlar - they are not coming

al-mı-yorum - I am not taking
al-mı-yorsun - you are not taking
al-mı-yor - he/she/it is not taking
al-mı-yoruz - we are not taking
al-mı-yorsunuz - you (pl.) are not taking
al-mı-yorlar - they are not taking

4.9 - The Negative with the Past Continuous Tense

gör-mü-yordum - I did not see
gör-mü-yordun - you did not see
gör-mü-yordu - he/she/it did not see
gör-mü-yorduk - we did not see
gör-mü-yordunuz - you did not see
gör-mü-yorlardı - they did not see

4.10 - The Aorist Tense in the Negative

The negative of the aorist tense is formed by adding a "-mez" or "-maz" to the verb stem. The "-z" is, however, omitted in the first person singular and plural

gel-me-m - I do not come
gel-mez-sin - you do not come
gel-mez - he/she/it does not come
gel-me-y-iz - we do not come ("-y-" is a buffer before the "-iz" aorist 1st
    person plural ending)
gel-mez-siniz - you (pl.) do not come
gel-mez-ler – they do not come

gel-mez-dim - I used to not come
gel-mez-din - you used to not come
gel-mez-di - he used to not come
gel-mez-dik - we used to not come

gel-mez-diniz - you (pl.) used to not come

gel-mez-lerdi / gel-mez-diler - they used to not come

4.11 - Positive and Negative Aorist Together Mean "as soon as"

The concept "as soon as" is expressed by combining the positive and the negative aorist bases.

> Ben mutfağa gir-er gir-mez, telefon çaldı - As soon as I entered the kitchen the telephone rang.
> Parayı al-ır al-maz arabayı satın aldı - As soon as he got the money he bought the car.
> Ben bir çay iste-r iste-mez çaycı getirdi - as soon as I wanted tea the teaman brought it.
> Olur olmaz - as soon as it happens.

Note, however, that the combination of the positive and negative aorist tense does not always mean "as soon as".

> İste-r iste-mez olacak - It is going to happen, like it or not.

"Olur olmaz" as an adjective can also mean "any old/just any.

> Bu olur olmaz adamın işi değil. - This job isn't for just anyone.

4.11 - The Formation of "cannot" or "to be unable to"

To communicate the concept of "cannot/to be unable to" an "-e/-a" is inserted before the aorist negative. This "-e/-a" receives a strong accent when speaking. This form is the negative of the suffix "-ebil/-abil" (see 11.1)

> gelmemek (not to come) > gel-e-memek (cannot come/ unable to come)
> gel-e-mi-yorum - I cannot come
> gel-e-me-diler - they couldn't come

4.12 - Words and Expressions Used to Form Negative Sentences

"Bir şey" (a thing, anything, nothing).

> Bir şey değil - It is nothing.
> Bir şey gör-me-dik - We didn't see anything.

"Bir türlü" (a sort, in no way, not at all)

> Bir türlü ol-ma-dı - It didn't happen at all.
> Bunu bir türlü anlamadım - I didn't understand this at all.

"Hiç" (nothing, ever, never)

> Bir hiç için sinirlendi - He got nervous/excited about nothing.
> Tanrı'nın önünde bir hiçim - Before God I am (a) nothing.
> Hiç iskender yediniz mi? - Have you ever eaten iskender?
> Hayir, hiç yemedim - No, I've never eaten (it).

"Hiçbir" (at all). Note the double negatives.

> Hiçbir şey gör-me-dim - I didn't see anything at all.
> Hiçbir şey bil-mez - He knows nothing at all.
> Hiçbir zaman gazete oku-maz - She never reads a newspaper.

"Kimse" (someone, anyone, nobody, no one)

> Kimse git-mi-yor - no one is going.
> Kimse var mı? - Is there anyone?
> Kimse yok - There is no one.

"Ne... ne..." (neither... nor)

> Ne Deniz'i ne Ayşe'yi gördüm - I saw neither Deniz nor Ayşe.
> Adam ne yakışklı ne çirkin - The man is neither handsome nor ugly.

Atasözü - Proverb

Damlaya damlaya göl olur.

Drop by drop forms (becomes) a lake

(All the little bits help)

Chapter 5

The Conditional

5.1 - The Verb "to be" in the Conditional

The conditional is formed around the word "ise". As an independent word it is not subject to vowel harmony. Note, however, that it is usually joined to the preceding word with vowel harmony (see 5.2 and 5.8).

isem - if I am   isek - if we are
isen - if you are   iseniz - if you all are
ise - if he/she/it is   iseler - if they are

Hasta isem - If I am sick.
Saat dokuz ise - If it is 9 o'clock.
Doktor ise yardım edecek - If he is a doctor he will help.
Kırmızı ise alırım - If it is red I'll take it.
Turist iseniz size gösteririm - If you are tourists I'll show you.

5.2 - Conditional Verbs

Conditional verbs are formed by adding the suffixed forms of "ise" to the various verb tenses. As a suffix it drops the "i" and is subject to vowel harmony.

geliyor-sam - if I am coming
geliyor-san - if you are coming
geliyor-sa - if he/she/it is coming
geliyor-sak - if we are coming
geliyor-sanız - if you (pl.) are coming
geliyor-larsa - if they are coming

With the future tense:

gidecek-sem - if I am going to go
gidecek-sen - if you are going to go
gidecek-se - if he/she/it is going to go
gidecek-sek - if we are going to go
gidecek-seniz - if you (pl.) are going to go
gidecekler-se/gidecek-seler - if they are going to go

5.3 - Likely and Less Likely Conditionals

The past conditional is made by adding "-ise" to either the past base or the simple past or aorist tense. Conditionals like this are open (i.e. there is a likely possibility that the action in question will take place).

görü-y-sem - if I saw OR
gördüm-se - if I saw.

If, however, you add the "-ise" suffix directly to the verb stem the possibility that the action in question will take place is less likely.

Senin yerinde ol-sam oraya gitmezdim - If I were in your place I wouldn't go there.
Kitabınızı almış ol-saydım onu geri verirdim. - If I had taken your book I'd have returned it.
Yarın gel-sem olmaz mı? - Could I not come tomorrow?

5.4 - Unfulfilled Conditional Sentences

There is also a type of conditional which communicates that there is no possibility of the condition being met. It is formed by adding the past tense of "olmak" (to be) to the normal conditional.

Fırsatım olmuş ol-saydı ondan vazgeçerdim - If I had had the chance I would have quit.
Herkes senin gibi yap-saydı, bize neler olurdu? - If everyone had behaved like you, what would have happened to us?

5.5 - Conditional Verb + "de/da" = "although"

If "-de/-da" follows the conditional verb the meaning becomes "although".

Kitabı dikkatle okudum-sa da, bir şey anlamadım - Although I read the book carefully I didn't understand a thing.

Kaçıyor-sa da yakalanacak - Although he is escaping, he will be apprehended.

5.6 - Whoever / Whatever and the Conditional

Sentences beginning with "whoever", "whatever", and "however" are formed with the conditional.

Ne yapmak ister-se yapacak - He will do whatever he wants to do.

Nasıl ister-sen öyle söyle - Say (it) however you wish.

5.7 - Other Ways In Which Conditionals Are Used

There are a couple of other ways of forming and using conditionals. The first is by forming a rhetorical question.

Ayşe gelmedi de kim geldi? - If Ayşe didn't come, who did?

Onu orada görmedi mi, burada arayacak - If he doesn't see it there he'll look here.

Turkish can use the conditional (often with an "-e/-a") to form a command or demand.

Bak-sana! - Do look!

Otur-sanıza - Do sit down!

Git-sene - Do go!

Bunu yap-sana - Do this!

The conditional suffix "-ise" can be used to draw attention to the preceding word.

Hikmet'se çalışkandır - As for Hikmet, he's industrious.

Ben-se hastayım - As for me, I'm sick.

5.8 - Some Examples of Conditional Sentences

Bunu yapacak-san, şimdi yap - If you are going to do it, do it now.

Bunu yapar-sam ölürüm - If I do that I'll die.

Siz gitmez-seniz, onlar da gidemezler - If you don't go they won't be able to go either.

Müşteri var-sa, bekle - If there is a customer, wait.

Kar yağ-sa da yağmaz-sa da Istanbul'a gidecek - Whether it snows or not, he is going to go to Istanbul.

bildiy-sem - if I knew

bil-seydim - had I known, or if only I had known

Bunu bil-seydim söylerdim - If I had known that, I would have said.

Ne ise - Well, anyway

Nerede-y-se (nerede ise) - soon, almost

Öyle-y-se (öyle ise) - in that case

Hiç olmaz-sa - at least

Ol-sa gerek - it must (logically) be

Bil-se bil-se o bilir - if anyone knows, he does.

The word "eğer" (if) sometimes introduces conditional sentences. It doesn't affect the meaning.

5.9 - The Slippery Word "And"

Although the dictionary translates the word "and" as "ve", it is not always used where we would use it in English. It can sometimes be replaced by a pause when speaking or a comma in writing. Sometimes the words "ile" (with) or "de/da" (also) are used where we would use "and".

Kardeşim, kızkardeşim ve ben - My brother, my sister and I.

Mavi, beyaz, kırmızı ve yeşil - Blue, white, red and green.

Güzel ve akıllı bir kız - A pretty and intelligent girl.

Çirkin ve huysuz bir adam - An ugly and ill-tempered man.

İstanbul'a gitti ve mal aldı - He went to Istanbul and got supplies.

"ile" (with) joins nouns or pronouns. It can stand alone or be suffixed. If suffixed it is subject to vowel harmony.

Mehmet ile Ahmet - Mehmet and Ahmet

Babam-la ben - My father and I

Sen-le biz - you and we

"de/da" orginally means "also", but can also mean "and", "too" and sometimes "but". It can also emphasize a preceding adverb. Unlike "ile", this word is subject to vowel harmony even if it stands alone.

Yaptım da anlamadım - I did it but didn't understand (it).

Mehmet de siz de - Both Mehmet and you.
O da yaptı - He did it too.
Ben de okudum - I read it also.

5.10 - Some Common Suffixes

"-ci" (or "-çi" when following an unvoiced consonant) shows adherence to a particular occupation or belief.

süt (milk) > süt-çü (milkman)
kapı (door, gate) > kapı-cı (doorman, porter, janitor)
eski (old) > eski-ci (rag-and-bone man)
dokuma (weaving) > dokuma-cı (weaver)
spor (sport) > spor-cu (sportsman)
yol (road) > yol-cu (traveller)
yalan (lie) > yalan-cı (liar)
inat (stubborn) > inat-çı (pig-headed)
milliyet (nationality) > milliyet-çi (nationalist)

"-li" = "with".   It is also used to create adjectives.

değer (value) > değer-li (valuable, with value)
akıl (intelligence) > akıl-lı (smart)

"-li" is also often (but not always) used to indicate nationality.

Nere-li-sin? - Where are you from?
Kanada-lı-y-ım - I am from Canada, I am Canadian.
Sen de ora-lı mısın? - Are you from there too?
Hayır, ben Amerika-lı-y-ım - No, I'm American.

"-siz" = without.

değer (value) > değer-siz (valueless)
akıl (intelligence) > akıl-sız (dumb, without intelligence)

"-ki" = who/which

Odamda-ki radyo - The radio which is in my room.
Bugün-kü gazete - Today's paper.
Orada-ki araba sizin mi? - Is the car over there yours?

Case endings are separated from "-ki" with a buffer "-n-".

> Benim-ki-n-den - from mine
> Onların-ki-ne baktım - I looked at theirs
> Sizin-ki-ni aldılar - they took yours

"ki" is also used as a separate word which can be translated as the conjunction "that". It is often used in sentences beginning with "öyle" or "o kadar" (so, so much) with the words "ki" was supposed to modify left to the imagination.

> O kadar yedik ki! - We ate so much (that I cannot begin to describe it!)
> O kadar çirkin bir yüzü var ki! - He's got such an ugly face (that I cannot begin to describe it!)

Note the way non-native speakers (often older people from non-Turkish minority groups) tend to use "ki" (in order to avoid using the Turkish participle) the way a native Turk would:

> Bir kadın ki, hep dedikodu yapar (awkward) > Hep dedikodu yapan bir kadın (right; see 9.2) - A woman who constantly gossips.

> Herkes bilir ki, Ahmet akıllı (awkward) > Herkes Ahmet'in akıllı olduğunu bilir (right; see 9.3) - Everyone knows that Ahmet is intelligent.

"-lik" = the most important use of "-lik" is to make abstract nouns:

> güzel (beautiful) > güzel-lik (beauty)
> çocuk (child) > çocuk-luk (childhood)
> akılsız (stupid) > akılsız-lık (stupidity)
> asker (soldier) > asker-lik (military service)
> yolcu (traveller) > yolcu-luk (journey)
> bir (one) > bir-lik (unit, unity, union)
> milliyetçi (nationalist) > milliyetçi-lik (nationalism)
> dokumacı (weaver) > dokumacı-lık (the weaver's trade)
> kim (who) >kim-lik (identity, identity card)

Another common use of "-lik" is to make adjectives and nouns from numerical expressions.

> yüz (hundred) > yüz-lük (hundred lira note)
> kişi (person) > üç kişi-lik (for three people)

gün (day) > iki gün-lük (two day)

seksen (eighty) > seksen-lik bir ihtiyar (old person of 80)

It also makes adjectives and nouns which show the purpose for which something is intended.

kitap (book) > kitap-lık (bookcase, library)

odun (wood) > odun-luk (woodshed, woodpile)

perde (curtain) > perde-lik (curtain material)

göz (eye) > göz-lük (glasses)

şimdi (now) > şimdi-lik (for now)

bugün (today) > bugünlük (for today)

"-iken" = "while" or "while being". When used as a suffix the "i" is often dropped or replaced by a "y" after vowels. It usually follows the aorist tense, though it can be attached to nouns as well.

Adana'ya gider-ken bir kitap okudum - While going to Adana I read a book.

Trene biner-ken Hüseyin'i gördüm - While getting on the train I saw Hussein.

Siz evde-y-ken biz çarşıya gittik - While you were at home we went to the market.

5.11 - Direct Speech, Uses of "Demek"

When direct speech is quoted it is either preceded or followed by "demek" (to say / to mean). If you put "demek" before the quotation it is followed by "ki", which is not translated. If "demek" comes after the quotation there is no "ki".

Dedi ki, "Belki" - He said, "Maybe".

"Belki," dedi - "Maybe," he said.

If a verb other than "demek" is used to describe a direct quotation (such as bağırmak - to shout), you introduce that word with "diye", a form of "demek".

"Gel!" diye bağırdı - He shouted, "Come!"

"Diye" also introduces unspoken thoughts.

Ne diye bize geldiniz? - What was the idea in coming to us?

Değişiklik olsun diye Marmaris'e gitti - For a change he went to Marmaris.

"Derken" = "while saying" also translates as "just as"

Ben haberi dinliyordum; derken komşum geldi. - Just as I was listening to the news, my neighbour came.

Atasözü - Proverb

İnsan ne ekerse onu biçer.

A man reaps what he sows.

Chapter 6

Adverbs

6.1 - Adverbs

Turkish doesn't make the distinction between adjectives and adverbs as clearly as English does.

"iyi" can mean both "good" and "well"

> Bu elbise sana iyi oturmadı - This dress doesn't suit you very well.
> Ali iyi bir çocuk - Ali is a good child.

Adverbs can be repeated for emphasis.

> Sık sık Adana'ya gidiyor - She often goes to Adana.
> Derin derin düşündüm - I thought deeply.
> Yavaş yavaş yürüyorlar - They are walking slowly.

The unaccented suffix "-ce/-ca" or "-çe/-ça" for unvoiced consonants also makes adverbs.

> güzel (beautiful) > güzel-ce (beautifully, properly)
> sade (simple) > sade-ce (simple, merely, only)
> doğru (direct) > doğru-ca (directly)
> bu (this) > bun-ca (in this way, this much; "n" buffer used with pronouns.

6.2 - Comparison of Adjectives and Adverbs

	"daha" (more)	"en" (most)
iyi - good	daha iyi - better	en iyi - best
kötü - bad	daha kötü - worse	en kötü - worst
tatlı - sweet	daha tatlı - sweeter e	n tatlı - sweetest
uzun - long	daha uzun - longer	en uzun - longest
güzel - nice	daha güzel - nicer	en güzel - nicest

44

çok - much	daha çok - more	en çok - most
az - little	daha az - less	en az - least.

The concept "than" is expressed by the suffix "-den/-dan". It makes "daha" unnecessary, although it may still be added for emphasis.

İstanbul, Ankara'dan büyüktür - Istanbul is bigger than Ankara.
Arabamız sizinkin-den güzeldir - Our car is nicer than yours.
En yararlı kitap İncil'dir - The most useful book is the New Testament.
Daha çok güç gerekiyor - More power is necessary.
Dünyanın en büyük nehri Amazon'dur - The world's biggest river is the
    Amazon.

6.3 - The Adverbs "here", "there" and "where" treated as Nouns

The Turkish equivalents to the adverbs "here", "there" and "where" are treated as nouns and, as such, they can take any noun-suffix.

Bura-da Ahmet oturuyor - Ahmet lives/sits here.
Bura-y-a geleceğim - I'm coming here.
Bura-dan ayrılıyor - He's leaving from this place.
Buralar-da - Around here, in these parts
Bura-sı güzel - This place is pretty
Bura-sı nere-si? - What place is this?

nere-de - in what place, where?
nere-y-e - to what place?
nere-den - from what place?

Nere-de kalıyorsunuz? - Where are you staying?
Nere-y-e gidiyor? - Where is he going?
Nere-den geliyorsun? - Where are you coming from?

şura-da, ora-da - in that place, there
şura-y-a, ora-y-a - to that place
şura-dan, ora-dan - from that place

Şura-da duruyor - He is standing there.
Şura-y-a gidiyor - He is going there.
Şura-dan ayrılıyor - He is leaving there.
Oralar-da - around there, in those parts.

6.4 - Adverbs of Place

içeri - inside
dışarı - outside
yukarı - up, upstairs
aşağı - down, downstairs
ileri - forward
geri - back, backwards, behind
öte - the far side, yonder
beri - the near side, hither

Odanın içerisi karanlık - The inside of the room is dark.
yukarı kat - the upper storey
Nehrin öte yakası - the other side of the river.

When indicating movement in a certain direction, these adverbs of place may be used with or without the dative "-e/-a".

Kız içeri / içeriye girdi - The girl went inside.
Ablam yukarı / yukarıya çıktı - My older sister went upstairs.

When the locative "-de/-da" or dative "-den/-dan" suffixes are added to "içeri", "dışarı", "yukarı" and "ileri", the final vowel sometimes disappears.

İçer(i)de çay içiyorduk - We were drinking tea inside. Dışar(ı)dan bir ses geldi - A sound came from outside. Yukar(ı)da Allah var - Up (there) God exists.
Öteye git - Go to the other (side).

6.5 - Some Adverbial Suffixes

There are a number of adverbial suffixes which can be added to verb stems.

"-erek/-arak" (doing/by doing) shows action which accompanies or goes just ahead of that described by the main verb.

Zehir iç-erek intihar etmiş - He committed suicide by drinking poison.
İsteme-y-erek oradan ayrıldı - We left from there unwillingly (the "-y-" is a buffer).
Gülümse-y-erek yanıt verdi - He answered smilingly (the "-y-" is a buffer).

With "olmak" this suffix means "as", "by", "by way of" or "as being".

46

Bunu sana bir arkadaş ol-arak söylüyorum -I'm telling you this as a friend.

İlk ol-arak kahveye gitti. - First of all he went to the coffee house.

"ince/ünce/ınca/unca" (on doing/when doing/while/when) shows action which has taken place just before the main verb. It has the same meaning as the personal participle ending "-ığında" (geldiğimde, yaptığımda; see 9.5)

Odamdan bak-ınca Ali'yi gordüm - When looking from my room I saw Ali.

Onu gör-ünce şaşırdım - On seeing him I was surprised.

Yaz ol-unca sıcak olur - When it becomes summer it becomes hot.

"-e -e/-a -a". When a pair of verb stems each has the suffix "-e -e/-a -a" attached, the action is emphasized or repeated.

Bil-e bil-e onu öldürmüş - He killed him deliberately (knowingly).

Koş-a koş-a geldi - He came running.

Sor-a sor-a Bağdat bulunur. - With constant asking you can find Baghdad (proverb).

Gül-e gül-e - (go) smilingly, goodbye.

Although the "-e -e / -a -a" is sometimes interchangeable with "-erek/ -arak" the two differ in that "-erek/-arak" does not connote repeated action. You can also add "-e -e / -a -a" to two different but related verb stems.

Öksür-e hapşır-a eczaneye gitti - Coughing and sneezing he went to the pharmacy.

"-inceye kadar/dek" or **"-ene kadar/dek"** (until)

Mustafa gel-inceye kadar gitmedim - I didn't go until Mustafa arrived.

Yağmur bit-inceye dek bekledim - I waited until it stopped raining.

"-meden/-madan" (without, before). Accent the syllable before this suffix.

Öğretmene sor-madan ayrılmam - I cannot leave without asking the teacher.

Para ol-madan hiçbir yere gidemeyeceğim -1 will not be able to go anywhere without money.

Gör-meden yargılama! - Don't judge before seeing!

"-dikten sonra/-tikten sonra" (after)

> Müdürle konuş-tuktan sonra durumu anladım - After speaking with the director I understood the situation.

"-eli, eli beri, eliden beri" (since)

> Türkiye'ye gel-eli altı ay oldu - It has been six months since he came to Turkey.
> Buraya geldim gel-eli... - Since I came here...
> Arabamdan çıktı çık-alı... - Since he stepped out of my car...

"-dik-çe/-tikçe" (the more). Can be used in conjuction with "her" (every).

> İnsan yaşlan-dıkça yavaşlıyor - The older one gets the more one slows down.
> Onu her gör-dükçe daha çok nefret ediyorum - The more I see it, the more I hate it.
> git-tikçe - the more it goes (also means "gradually")
> ol-dukça - the more it happens (also means "rather, quite, quite a lot")

"-meksizin" (without)

> Beni gör-meksizin gitti - He left without seeing me.

"-mektense" (rather than)

> Sinemaya git-mektense, balkonda oturup sohbet edelim - Rather than go to the cinema, let's sit on the balcony and chat.

6.6 - Some Adverbs of Time

"artık" (at last, from now on)

> Artık tatil başladı -At last the holiday has started.
> Artık onu ziyaret etmem - From now on I'm not going to visit her.

"daha" (still, yet, again)

> Daha gelmedi mi? - Has he not arrived yet?
> Adam daha burada mı? - Is the man still here?
> Bir saat daha beklemeli - It's necessary that he wait one more hour.
> Bunu bir daha yapmayın! - Don't do that again!

"gene, yine" (again, still)

Gene şikayet etmeye başladı - He's started to complain again.

"hemen" (at once, just, as soon as)

İstiklâl Marşı başlayınca hemen ayağa kalktık - We stood up at once
  when the national anthem started.
Haberi duyunca hemen hastaneye gittim - I went to the hospital as soon
  as I heard the news.

Note: a repeated "hemen" is a little less precise.
  Kitabı okumayı hemen hemen bitirdim - I have read nearly all of the
  book.

"henüz" (just now, not just yet)

Henüz evden çıkmıştım - I had just left home.
Ahmet bir saat once gelmiş, kendisini henüz görmedim - Ahmet came an
  hour ago, I haven't seen him yet.

6.7 - The conjunction "-mek + üzere"

"Üzere", which means "on", is used with the infinitive "mek" form of verbs to
mean "so as to/in order to", "on condition that", or "on the point of".

Öğrenciler sınavı kazanmak üzere hazırlanıyorlar - The students are
  getting ready in order to pass the test.
Haftaya geri vermek üzere bu bilgisayarı alıyorum - I am taking this
  computer on condition that I give it back next week.
Yola çıkmak üzereyiz - We are on the point of leaving.

"Olmak üzere" also appears in conjuction with numbers to mean "being" or
"as being". It can be omitted when translating into English.

Üç tanesi eski, dört tanesi yeni olmak üzere yedi şapkam var - I have
  seven hats, three of them old and four of them new.

Atasözü - Proverb

Karı koca ipek, araya giren kopek.

A husband and wife are silk, he who comes between them is a dog.

7

Adjectives

7.1 - Intensification of Adjectives

You can intensify adjectives by repetition as we saw in 6.1, or by prefixing a syllable which resembles the first syllable of the word but ends in an "m", "p", "s" or "r". There is no rule of thumb by which one can deduce which letter to use. Note that in speech this prefix is accented.

> başka (other) > bambaşka (totally different)
> ayrı (different) > apayrı (completely different)
> doğru (straight) > dosdoğru (dead straight)
> yeni (new) > yepyeni (brand new)
> bütün (whole) > büsbütün (completely, entirely)
> düz (straight) > dümdüz (perfectly straight)
> temiz (clean) > tertemiz (spotless)
> siyah (black) > simsiyah (pitch black)
> beyaz (white) > bembeyaz (perfectly white)
> kırmızı (red) > kıpkırmızı (bright red)
> yeşil (green) > yemyeşil (bright green)
> sarı (yellow) > sapsarı (bright yellow)
> mavi (blue) > masmavi (bright blue)

7.2 - Some Quantifying Adjectives

başka, diğer - other
> başkası/bir başka - another one, someone else başkaları - some others
> Bu kitabı benden değil, başkasından aldılar - They did not get this book from me, (but) from others.

bazı/kimi/kimisi - some, someone (the "ı" of "bazı" is not a suffix, it is part of the word)

      bazı/kimi insanlar - some people

      bazıları/kimileri - some of them

      bazılarımız/kimimiz - some of us

      Kimi gül, kimi lale sever - Some like roses, some like tulips.

biraz - a little

      Biraz tuz verir-misiniz? - Will you give me a little (bit of) salt?

birkaç - a few, several

      Birkaç kalem kayboldu - A few pens were lost.

birçok - many, quite a few

      Depremde birçok ev çöktü - Many houses collapsed during the quake.

bütün - whole, all

      bütün gün - the whole day

      Bütün kitabı okudum - I read the whole book.

      Bütün gün çalıştım - I worked the whole day.

çok - many, much

      çoğu - most

      Parası çok - He's got much money.

      çoğumuz - most of us

      çoğu zaman - most of the time

      çoğu adam - most men

hep - all, wholly, always, entirely, still

      hepimiz - all of us

      hepiniz - all of you

      hepsi - all of them / it / everybody

      hep öyle - always the same

her - every

      her gün - every day

      her yerde - everywhere

      her zaman - always

      herkes - everyone

      herhangi - any

      her ikisi - both of them

öbür - the other

>öbürü - the other one
>
>Yarın öbür gün Ankara'ya gidiyor - Tomorrow (or) the next day he's
>going to Ankara.
>
>Öbürünü tercih ederim - I prefer the other one.
>
>öbür dünya - the next world

7.3 - Kendi - self/own

"Kendi" is used as an adjective. It can take the possessive suffix to emphasize the concept of myself, yourself, etc. It is also used in a reflexive sense.

>kendi odam - my own room
>
>kendi evin - your own house
>
>kendi köyümüz - our own village
>
>Bunu kendim yaptım - I did this all by myself.
>
>Siz kendiniz - you yourselves
>
>Kendi kendime, "Peter, hastasın", dedim. - I said to myself,
>"Peter, you're sick".
>
>Kendi kendinizi suçlamayın - Don't blame yourselves.
>
>Kendiliğinden - of its/her/his own accord, by its/her/him self
>
>Kendisi is a polite alternative to "o" (he/she).

7.4 - The Suffix "-sel" Turns Nouns into Adjectives

>bölge (region) > bölgesel (regional)
>
>gelenek (tradition) > geleneksel (traditional)
>
>kimya (chemistry) > kimyasal (chemical)
>
>Tanrı (God) > tanrısal > (divine)

7.5 - Suffixes Used to Create Nouns or Adjectives from Verb Stems

"-ç"

>iğrenmek (to feel loathing) > igrenç (loathsome)
>
>kazanmak (to win) > kazanç (profit)
>
>sevinmek (to be pleased) > sevinç (joy)

"-ek/-ak"

>batmak (to sink) > batak (marsh)
>
>durmak (to stop) > durak (bus stop)
>
>konmak (to settle) > konak (place to stay)

"-gen/-gan"

    atılmak (to be thrown) > atılgan (reckless, outgoing)
    çekinmek (to withdraw) > çekingen (shy)
    dövüşmek (to fight) > dövüşken (bellicose)
    unutmak (to forget) > unutkan (forgetful)

"-gi/-gı"

    çalmak (to play) > çalgı (instrument)
    çizmek (to draw) > çizgi (line)
    duymak (to hear, to feel) > duygu (feeling)
    sermek (to spread out) > sergi (display, fair)
    yazmak (to write) > yazgı (destiny, fate)

"-gin/-gın"

    girmek (to enter) > girgin (sociable)
    kaçmak (to flee) > kaçkın (fugitive)
    kesmek (to cut) > keskin (sharp)
    uymak (to conform) > uygun (suitable)

"-u/-ü/-i/-ı"

    koşmak (to run) > koşu (race)
    ölmek (to die) > ölü (corpse)
    ölçmek (to measure) > ölçü (measurement)
    yapmak (to make) > yapı (construction)
    yazmak (to write) > yazı (writing)

"-uk/-ük/-ik/-ık"

    açmak (to open) > açık (open)
    bozmak (to destroy) > bozuk (corrupt, broken)
    karışmak (to mix, to be confused) > karışık (disordered, mixed up)

"-um/-üm/-im/-ım"

    basmak (to press, to print) > basım (printing)
    dağıtmak (to distribute) > dağıtım (distribution)
    demek (to say) > deyim (saying, expression)
    doğmak (to be born) > doğum (birth)
    durmak (to stand) > durum (situation)
    ölmek (to die) > ölüm (death)
    yatırmak (to deposit) > yatırım (investment)
    yazmak (to write) > yazım (spelling)
    yönetmek (to administer) > yönetim (administration)

"untu/-üntü-ıntı/-inti"

akmak (to flow) > akıntı (current)
çıkmak (to come out) > çıkıntı (projection)
süpürmek (to sweep) > süprüntü (sweepings)
sarsmak (to shake) > sarsıntı (tremor)

"-m"

anlamak (to understand) > anlam (meaning)
kavramak (to grasp) > kavram (concept)

Atasözü - Proverb

Öğrenmenin yaşı yoktur

One is never too old to learn

Chapter 8

Interrogatives and Imperatives

8.1 - The "ne" Interrogative

The word "ne" (what) occurs in many forms and is used in a variety of ways.

nerede - where
nereye - to where
nereden - from where
nereli - belonging to where
niçin (ne için) - why
neci - of what profession
ne kadar - how much
ne zaman - when
ne gibi/tür/biçim - what sort of
nasıl (ne asıl) - how/what kind of

As seen above "ne" may take case endings but it usually remains in the absolute form when it is the object of a verb.

Ne gördünüz? - What did you see?
Ne istiyorsun? - What do you want?

The definite objective case "neyi" is used instead of "ne"when a compound of "ne" follows or when you refer to a specific thing.

Neyi nerede gördün? - What did you see (and) where?
Ne okudunuz? - What did you read? (answer: bir kitap - a book)
Neyi okudunuz? - What did you read? (answer: the name of the book being read)

Note the following:
Neyin var? - What's the matter with you?

Neme lazım - What's it got to do with me? ("Bana ne" expresses the
same thing and is more common.)
Neler yaptı! - What things he did!
Ne karıştırıyorsunuz? - what are you intervening for?
Ne tatlı! - How sweet!

Note that "niye" (for "neye") and "neden" both mean "why" but that "neden"
is also a noun meaning "cause/reason".

8.2 - Other Interrogatives

"Kim" (who), "hangi" (which) and "kaç" (how much/how many) take
possessive suffixes. "Kim" (who) may also take any case endings as well as
the plural suffix. Note that the noun which "kaç" modifies is singular.

Çantayı kim-e verdiniz? - To whom did you give the bag?
Kim-i vurdun? - Whom did you hit?
Parayı kim-den çaldı? - From whom did he steal the money?
Kim-leri gördünüz? - Whom all did you see?
Bu palto kim-in? - Whose coat is this?
Kim-in-le birlikte geldiler? - With whom did they come?
Kim-iniz? - Who among you?
Siz hangi ülkeden geldiniz? - Which country did you come from?
Hangi okula gittiler? - To which school did they go?
Hanginiz? - Which of you?

Kaç yaşındasın? - How old are you?
Kaç kişisiniz? - How many of you are there?
Bu kitaplanın kaçı bizim? - How many of these books are ours?
Ayın kaçında gelecekler? - On which day of the month are they going to
come?

8.3 - Telling the time

Saat kaç? - What time (hour) is it? (The hour how many?)
Saat üç - Three o'clock.
Saat üçü sekiz geçiyor - Eight past three.
Saat üçe on var - Ten to three.
Saat üçü çeyrek geçiyor - Quarter past three.
Saat üçe çeyrek var - Quarter to three.

Saat üçe on kala gelir - It comes at ten to three.
Saat üçü on geçe gider - It goes as ten past three.

Saat üçü çeyrek geçe kalkar - It departs at a quarter past three.
Saat üçe çeyrek kala varır - It arrives at a quarter to three.

Yarımda (at the half) refers to 12:30 PM.

8.4 - Money, Weights and Measures

The Turkish currency is called the "lira" (TL for short). It is divided into 100 "kuruş".

Kaç kuruş? - how many kuruş? (used somewhat jokingly when something is expected to be really cheap).
Kaç para? - How much money? (i.e How much does it cost?)
Kaç lira? - How many liras?

Since 1932 Turkey has used the Metric system. Two older terms that one still comes across on occasion are the "arşın" (about 68 centimeters) and the "okka" (1283 grams). Sometimes the kilogram is referred to as an "okka".

santimetre or santim - centimeter
metre - meter
kilometre - kilometer
kilo or kilogram - kilogram
litre - liter
bir kilometre kare - one square kilometer
bir metre küp - one cubic meter
bir dönüm - 1000 square meters (about 1/4 of an acre)

8.5 - The Interrogative Particle

Questions are formed by putting "mi/mı/mu/mü" after words. Although it is written and spoken as a separate word, its vowel varies according to vowel harmony as if it were a suffix. Note that unlike English, Turkish sentences do not tend to rise in tone when asking yes/no questions. In fact the emphasis is often (but not always) on the suffix previous to the interrogative particle, with the voice dropping on the interrogative particle itself.

Uçak mı? - Is it an airplane?
Kesin mi? - Is it certain?
Çocuk mu? - Is it a child?
Çok düşük mü? - Is it very low?
Hasta mı? - Is he sick?

57

You can add the personal pronoun endings to it in conjunction with nouns and adjectives.

> Hasta mı-sın? - Are you sick?
> Öğretmen mi-siniz? - Are you (pl.) teachers?

With present tense verbs it is placed after the "yor" except in the third person plural, where it follows the "lar". Although not always directly attached to the verb, it is still subject to vowel harmony.

> Geliyor mu-sun? - Are you (sing.) coming?
> Gelmiyor mu-sunuz? - Are you (pl.) not coming?
> Gidecekler mi? - Are they going?

The Aorist tense is often used in polite questions.

> Görür mü-sünuz? - Do you see?/Will you see?
> Görür mü-y-dün? - Did you used to see?
> Gitmez mi-y-im? - Do I not go?
> Bakmaz mı-y-ım? - Do I not look?
> Bir kitap verir mi-siniz? - Will you give (me) a book.
> Asansörü tamir eder mi-siniz? - Will you fix the elevator?

8.6 - The Imperative

The verb stem forms the imperative (i.e., simply drop the "-mek" from the infinitive "dictionary" form of the verb).

> Dinle! - Listen!
> Otur! - Sit!
> Konuş! - Speak!
> Git! - Go!
> Girme! - Don't enter!
> Koşma! - Don't run!
> Konuşma! - Don't speak!

Adding the personal endings directly to the verb stem makes the command more polite.

> Oturun - sit!
> Oturmayın - don't sit!
> Gidiniz - Go!

58

Gitmeyiniz - Don't go!

The third person imperative is made by adding "-sin/-sün/-sın/-sun" (depending on vowel harmony) to the verb stem.

Git-sin - Let him/her/it go.
Git-sinler - Let them go.
Gitme-sin - Don't let him/her/it go.
Gitme-sinler - Don't let them go.

Otur-sun - Let him/her/it sit.
Oturma-sın - Don't let him/her/it sit

İç-sin - Let him drink
İçme-sin - Don't let him drink

There are some useful expressions based on the imperative form of "olmak" (to be).

Sağol (sağ + ol) - Be well (alternative to "teşekkür ederim" - thank you).
Geçmiş olsun - Let it be past (said when someone is sick or in trouble).
Eksik olma - Don't be wanting (response to a favour).
Oh olsun - Let there be "oh" (i.e, serves you/him/her right).
Afiyet olsun - Let there be health (used like the French "bon appetit").

8.7 - Buyurun!

"Buyurmak" means "to command". "Buyur" or, more common, "Buyurun!" ("Command!") may mean something like, "come in", "help yourself or "sit down". It is often used where we would use the word "welcome" in English.

Buyurun - Welcome
Bize buyurmaz mısınız? - Won't you honour us with a visit?
Ne buyurdunuz? - What did you say? (extremely polite)
Buyurun, kahveniz - Here is your coffee.
Buyurun, arabaya - Kindly enter the car.

Atasözü – Proverb
Sana vereyim bir öğüt, kendi ununu kendin öğüt.
Let me give you some advice: grind your own flour
(If you want a thing done well, do it yourself)

Chapter 9

Participles and Verbal Nouns

9.1 - Introductory Comments on Participles and Verbal Nouns

Participles are simply adjectives made from verbs. In English we have two types of participles: past participles and present participles (i.e. the food is cooking and the food is cooked). In English, however, present participles share the "-ing" ending with verbal nouns. Note the difference in the use of the following two usages of the word "reading". In "Her sister is reading" the word "reading" is a present participle in whose place you can put other adjectives (e.g. Her sister is skinny). On the other hand, in "Her hobby is reading", the word "reading" is a noun (a verbal noun to be exact) in whose place you can put other nouns (e.g. Her hobby is music).

In Turkish, present participles and verbal nouns have different suffixes. Present participles, as we will see, end in "-en/-an" or "-yen/-yan" while there are a number of ways in which to form verbal nouns.

9.2 - Forming Present Participles

In Turkish participles are used where English would use a relative clause (i.e. a clause beginning with "who", "which", or "that"). As noted in 9.1, present participles are formed by adding "-en/-an" or "-yen/-yan" to the verb stem, depending on whether or not it ends in a vowel.

olmak (to become, to be, to happen) > ol-an - becoming, being,
  happening; who or which becomes/is/happens
almak (to take, to receive) > al-an - taking, receiving, who receives
gitmek (to go) > gid-en - going, who goes
yürümek (to walk) > yürü-yen - walking, who or which walks

Note that the present participle communicates action which happens at the same time as the main verb of the sentence, so it may be translated in the past, present or future tenses.

Oyna-yan çocuklar yoruldular - The children who were playing got tired.

Oyna-yan çocuklar yoruluyorlar - The children who are playing are getting tired.

Oyna-yan çocuklar yorulacaklar - The children who are playing will get tired.

The present participle can be used as a noun. For instance, instead of "bunu yapan insanlar" (people who do this) you can say "bunu yapanlar" (those who do this).

Çay iste-y-en var mı? - Is there anyone who wants tea?
Mağaraya gir-en kaybolur - He who enters the cave gets lost.
Sigara iç-en cezalandırılacak - He who smokes will be punished
çalış-anlar - those who work
meşgul ol-an - he who is busy
işi olma-y-an - he who has no work

9.3 - Personal Participles

As we have seen, the "-en/-an/-yen/-yan" based present participles described above are used when English would use a relative pronoun (i.e, "who", "which", "what", "that") as the subject of the relative clause. In other types of relative clauses, however, Turkish uses a beautiful construction formed by adding "-dik/-dük/ -dık/-duk" to the root stem. Remember that the "k" become a "ğ" when followed by a vowel.

okumak - to read
oku-duğ-um gazete - the newspaper which I read
oku-duğ-un gazete - the newspaper which you (sing.) read
oku-duğ-u gazete - the newspaper which he/she read
oku-duğ-umuz gazete - the newspaper which we read
oku-duğ-unuz gazete - the newspaper which you (plural) read
oku-duk-ları gazete - the newspaper which they read

kal-dığ-ın otel - the hotel in which you stay/stayed
yap-tığ-ımız iş - the work which we do/have done
otur-duğ-um ev - the house in which I live/lived
oku-duğ-u kitap - the book which he is reading/read
gör-düğ-ünüz adam - the man whom you see/saw

Note that the above examples communicate either the present or past tense. In the future tense the future participle "-ecek/acak" is used.

> kal-acağ-ın hotel - the hotel in which you are going to stay
> yap-acağ-ımız iş - the work which we are going to do
> otur-acağ-ım ev - the house in which I am going to live
> oku-y-acağ-ı kitap - the book which he is going to read
> yaz-acak-ları rapor - the report which they are going to write

Here are some sample sentences:

> Geçen hafta git-tiğim lokanta Beyoğlu'ndaydı. - The restaurant I went to last week was in Beyoğlu.
> Otur-duğunuz daire ucuz mu? - It the apartment you are living in cheap?
> Sana ver-diğim kitap güzel miydi? - Was the book I gave you good?
> İste-diğin kadar git - Go as far as as you want.
> İzmir'e git-tiğimiz zaman hava berbattı. - When we went to Izmir the weather was terrible.
> Çocuklar oyna-dıkları zaman gürültü yaparlar - Children make noise when they play.
> Yakala-ya-ma-yacagımız maymun - The monkey we will be unable to catch. (Isn't Turkish wonderful?)

If "halde" follows the personal participle it means "although" or "in a state of, if "üzere" follows the personal participle it means "as", and if "yerde" follows the personal participle it means "instead of".

> Bunu bil-diğim halde bir şey yapamıyorum. - Although I know that I can't do anything.
> Kapıda yazıl-dığı üzere - As is written on the door...
> Burada üşü-y-ecegimiz yerde, taksiye binelim - Instead of getting cold here let's take a taxi.

9.4 - The Personal Participle as a Noun Phrase

Personal participles can also be used where English uses noun phrases.

> İstanbul'a git-tiğini kimse bilmiyor - No one knows that he has gone to Istanbul.
> Hasta ol-acağ-ınız-dan şüphem yok - I don't doubt that you will get sick.

9.5 - The Personal Participle with Case Endings

62

The personal participle with "-den/-dan/-ten/-tan" means "for", "because" or "due to"

> Hiçbir şey görme-diğim-den sustum - Because I didn't see anything I kept quiet.

Note that you can also use the word "için" (for, because, due to) to communicate the same idea.

> Hiçbir şey görme-diğim için sustum - Because I didn't see anything I kept quiet.
> Buraya gel-diğim için zorluk çekiyorum - I am having a difficult time because I came here.

The personal participle with "-de/-da" means "when" or "upon".

> Seni gor-düğüm-de çok sevindim - I was really happy when I saw you.
> Bunu gazetede oku-duğum-da üzüldüm - Upon reading that in the paper I became sad.

The personal participle with "-e/-a" means "instead of". "-e/ -a" with "göre" means "since" or "in view of the fact".

> Karakola gid-eceğin-e hastaneye gitti - Instead of going to the police station he went to the hospital.
> Kitabı oku-duğun-a göre bunu bilmek zorundasın - In view of the fact that you have read the book you must know this.

9.6 - The Personal Participle as Indicator of Indirect Speech

A very important use of the personal participle is to indicate indirect speech.

> Ali'ye Ankara'ya yarın gid-eceğimi söyledim - I told Ali that I would go to Ankara tomorrow, (the "-i" on the end of "gideceğimi" is the accusative case ending. It is the object of   the verb "söylemek" (to say)).

> Onu ne kadar sev-diğimi anlattım - I explained how much I love her.

9.7 - The Perfect Participle

The "-miş" suffix added to verb stems in conjuction with the future tense forms the perfect participle. Because this "-miş" ending looks the same as the "hearsay" tense (see 10.1), it is easy to confuse them.

Yapmış olacağim -1 shall have done that.
Gitmiş olacak - He shall have gone.

9.8 - The Verbal Noun

There are basically three ways to form verbal nouns (i.e. nouns which describe an action or experience). They are formed by the suffixes "-mek/mak", "-me/ma", and "-(y)iş/üş/ış/uş". The most common verbal noun is the "dictionary" infinitive "-mek/mak" form. It remains in its absolute form when it is the object of "istemek" (to want) and, rarely, "bilmek" (to know).

Ankara'ya gitmek istiyorum - I want to go to Ankara.
Kahve içmek istiyorum - I want to drink coffee.
Seni görmek istiyorum - I want to see you.
Türkiye hakkında her şeyi öğrenmek istiyorum - I want to learn
    everything about Turkey.
Susmak bilmiyor - He doesn't know how to shut up.

You can, however, also use the normal definite objective case.

Ankara'ya gitmeyi istiyorum - I want to go to Ankara. (Grammatically
    correct, but considered poor Turkish).
Okumayı biliyorum - I know how to read.
Yüzmeyi biliyor - He knows how to swim.

The only common case endings the "-mek/mak" verbal noun can take are the locative ("bilmek-te", "olmak-ta") and the ablative ("bilmek-ten", "olmak-tan"). It cannot be put into the genitive or possessive cases. The locative form is a rather formal way to form the simple present or past tense. It can also mean "was in the act of...".

Galatasaray şimdi Amsterdam'da futbol oynamakta - Galatasaray (name
    of Turkish soccer team) is now playing soccer in Amsterdam.
Beşiktaş (another soccer team) dün Paris'te futbol oynamaktaydı -
    Beşiktaş was playing soccer in Paris yesterday.

9.9 - The "-me/ma" Verbal Noun

The most common use of the "-me/-ma" form of the verbal noun is to indicate what is wanted when asking for or ordering something. It is formed by adding "-me/-ma" to the verb root (or by simply dropping the "-k" from the infinitive "-mek/-mak" form of the verb). It is combined with a personal suffix.

> Koltukta otur-ma-nı söyledi - He told you to sit in the chair.
> Ahmet annesine telefon et-me-mi istiyordu - Ahmet wanted me to phone his mother.
> Yolcuların sigara iç-me-mesi rica olunur - It is requested that the passengers not smoke.
> Uçağın kalk-ma-sını bekliyoruz - We're waiting for the plane to take off.

The "-me/ma" verbal nouns can also be used as qualifiers, as adjectives and as nouns which result from a certain action.

> git-me zamanı - time to go
> dol-ma biber - stuffed pepper
> otur-ma odası - sitting room
> dön-me - someone who converted to another religion

Sometimes the only way to distinguish this verbal noun from the negative "-me" (see 4.3) is from the context. "Bilmem" can mean "my knowing" (verbal noun) or "I don't know" (aorist negative tense). "Bakmam" can mean "my looking" (verbal noun) or "I don't look" (aorist negative tense).

With verbs other than "istemek" (to want) and "bilmek" (to know) the appropriate case ending is added to the "-me/ma" infinitive form.

> Oku-ma-yı severim - I like reading.
> Adana'ya git-me-yi düşünüyorum - I'm thinking about going to Adana.
> Türkçe öğren-me-ye çalışıyorum - I'm trying to learn Turkish.
> Sizi gör-me-ye geldik - we came to see you.

By adding the negative suffix "-me" you get the following:

> gel-me-me - not coming
> Onun gel-me-me-si beni şaşırtıyor - His not coming surprises me.

9.10 - The "-iş/uş/ış/üş" Verbal Noun

The original idea behind the verbal noun ending "-iş", was to illustrate the way something is done. Unfortunately, that is not always evident.

görmek (to see) > gör-üş (way of seeing things, outlook)
yürümek (to walk) > yürü-y-üş (way of walking, gait)
almak + vermek (to take + to give) > alışveriş (shopping) göstermek (to show) > gösteriş (ostentation)

gösteriş-siz - plain, simple, not ostentatious.

Adamın yürü-y-üş-ü cok garip - The man's way of walking is very
    strange.

Atasözü - Proverb

Sabreden derviş muradina ermiş.

The patient dervish has reached his goal.

Chapter 10

More on Verbs

10.1 - The "Hearsay" Tense

Turkish has an interesting tense form based on the suffix "-miş/-imiş" which doesn't communicate time so much as the fact that the information which the speaker is communicating is not known with absolute certainty. In other words, the speaker was not an eyewitness to the event he/she is describing. Although this same suffix is used with the perfect participle in the future tense (see 9.7; 10.2) it is something altogether different. When used in the "hearsay" tense, the "-miş/-imiş" suffix means "reportedly is/was" as in: "it seems/seemed he is/was..." or "I gather that he/she/it is/was...".

The "hearsay" tense may be combined with any other tense, except the past "-di". It may also be used with the word "gibi" (like, resembles). The two words in conjuction then mean "as though".

> Annesi aşçı imiş / Annesi aşçı-y-mış - They say that his mother is a cook.

In the first example the "imiş" stands alone, and in the second example it is attached to "aşçı" (cook). Because it is attached the rules of vowel harmony(-miş/-müş/-mış/-muş) apply.

> Hava yağmurlu olacak-mış - They say it's going to rain.
> Arabayla gidecek-miş - They say he's going by car.
> Ben onu vur-muş-um! - I'm supposed to have shot him ("Vur-muş-muş-um) is also possible.
> Gidecek-miş gibi arabasına bindi - He stepped into his car as though he was leaving.

> Ekmek iyi kızar-mış - the bread is well toasted. (It is well toasted as a result of action which preceded it, but the fact that it is well toasted is something you only realized when you got to the table. If you had

been standing over the toaster while the bread was toasting you would have said, "Ekmek iyi kızardı".)

10.2 - "-Miş" as a Perfect Participle

As we have already seen in 9.7, the "-miş" suffix also serves as a perfect participle ending when it is attached to the stems of verbs other than "olmak" (to be). Remember that the perfect participle describes a present state arising out of past action.

> "Ahmet geldi" - Ahmet came (simple past tense) > Ahmet gel-miş - Ahmet has come (perfect participle). (Of course "Ahmet gel-miş" could also mean "I'm told that Ahmet has come".)

"-miş" as a perfect participle suffix differs from the "-miş/ -imiş" "hearsay" suffix in that it is exclusively a past and never a present tense, and that it doesn't imply a lack of first-hand knowledge.

The English future perfect tense (I shall have gone) is translated by the perfect participle plus the future of olmak.

> Git-miş olacağim - I shall have gone.

10.3 - The Pluperfect (Past Perfect) Tense

The pluperfect tense (also known as the past perfect tense) indicates that one action preceded another in the past. It is formed by adding the simple past tense endings to the perfect participles. It is much more common in Turkish than it is in English. Note that this tense does not have the "hearsay" quality often associated with the "-miş" endings.

> ol-muş-tum - I had become
> al-mış-tın - you had bought
> bil-miş-tik - we had known
> gör-müş-lerdi - they had seen

> Arabayı beş yıl önce al-mış-lardı, geçen hafta sattılar. - They had bought the car five years ago and sold it last week.

10.4 - "-Dir" Also Used to Communicate Uncertainty.

The suffix "-dir" can be added to the first and second persons of the present tense to communicate the fact that the speaker is not 100% certain of what he/she is saying. This form is often used by radio and T.V. presenters. Note that "-dir" is affected by vowel harmony.

Misafirimizin başına gelenleri hepiniz biliyorsunuz-dur - You all know what has happened to our guest.

10.5 - The Perfect Conditional Tense

The perfect conditional tense is formed by adding the "-isem" suffixes to the perfect participle.

Kapadokya'yı görmüş-se-niz, şanlısınız - If you have seen Cappadocia your are lucky.

10.6 - Passive Forms of the Verb

A verb is passive when it receives rather than does the action. When a verb is put in the passive, its former object becomes the subject (i.e. "I caught the ball" > "The ball was caught".)

The passive verb stems are formed in one of three ways:

1. by inserting "-il/-ül/-ıl/-ul" to verbs whose stems end in any consonant except "l"
2. by inserting "-in/-ın/-ün/-un" to verbs whose stems ends in an "1"
3. by inserting an "-n" to verb stems which end in a vowel

yapmak (to do) > yap-ıl-mak (to be done)
görmek (to see) > gör-ül-mek (to be seen)
tatbik etmek (to apply) > tatbik ed-il-mek (to be applied)
almak (to take) > al-ın-mak (to be taken)
bilmek (to know) > bil-in-mek (to be known)
okumak (to read) > oku-n-mak (to be read)

There are a few exceptions:

ayırmak (to separate) > ayrılmak (te be separated)

çevirmek (to turn, to translate) > cevrilmek (to be turned, to be translated)

kaybetmek (to lose) > kaybolmak (to be lost)

To indicate who carried out the action of a passive verb the word "tarafından" or the adverbial suffix "-ce" can be used.

Bardak bebek tarafından kırıldı - The glass was broken by the baby.

Bu projeye başbakan-ca karar verildi - This project has been decided on by the prime-minister.

Turkish can make intransitive verbs passive. Since intransitive verbs don't have an object of the verb, they can't have a subject when they are put into the passive. In other words, they are used impersonally (without indicating person).

Havaalanına bu yoldan gidilir - Going to the airport is done by this road.

Burada yıkanılmaz - Here one doesn't wash oneself.

10.7 - Reflexive Forms of the Verb

Reflexive verbs are different from passive verbs in that they do not affect any object outside of themselves. The action is either done to oneself or on behalf of oneself. It is formed by:

1. inserting an "-n" to verbs whose stems end in a vowel
2. inserting an "-in" to verbs whose stems end in a consonant

yıkamak (to wash) > yıka-n-mak (to wash oneself)
söylemek (to say) > söyle-n-mek (to talk to oneself, to mumble)
çekmek (to pull) > çek-in-mek (to withdraw, to abstain)
bulmak (to find) > bul-un-mak (to find oneself, to be)
etmek (to do) > ed-in-mek (to acquire)
geçmek (to pass) > geç-in-mek (to get by, to make a living)
görmek (to see) > gör-ün-mek (to appear, to seem)

Obviously the passive and reflexive are identical in verbs which end in a vowel or an "l". This could be confusing in some cases. For instance, "kız yıkandı" could mean "the girl has washed herself" or "the girl has been washed". You can take away doubt by inserting the passive suffix "-il". "Kız yıkanıldı" (the girl has been washed). On the other hand, you can also say, "kız kendini yıkadı" (the girl washed herself. See 7.3).

10.8 - The Reciprocal Verb

Reciprocal (or cooperative) verbs are formed by adding "-ş/iş" to verb stems. This usually indicates that the action was done by more than one agent.

çarpmak (to hit) > çarp-ış-mak (to collide)
dövmek (to beat) > döv-üş-mek (to fight each other)
sevmek (to love) > sev-iş-mek (to make love)
oynamak (to play) > oyna-ş-mak (to play together)
görmek - to see > gör-üş-mek (to see each other)

There are a number of words which don't have an obvious reciprocal meaning yet utilize the "-ş/-iş" suffix.

gelmek (to come) > gel-iş-mek (to develop)
yetmek (to be sufficient, to be enough) > yet-iş-mek (to grow up, to
    catch up)

10.9 - The Subjunctive

The subjunctive is a verb form used to communicate the fact that the concept in question is not a reality but is either hoped for, wanted or feared. It is formed by inserting "-e/-a" after consonants and "-ye/-ya" after vowels; its personal endings are somewhat different from the regular personal endings.

olayım - may I be, let me be
olasın - may you be, let you be
olsun - may he/she/it be, let him be
olalım - may we be, let us be
olasınız - may you be, let you be
olsunlar - may they be, let them be

gideyim - may I go, let me go
gidesin - may you go, let you go
gitsin - may he/she/it go, let him go
gidelim - may we go, let us go
gidesiniz - may you go, let us go
gitsinler - may they go, let us go

Only the "I" and "we" forms are in common use.

Alayım - Let me take it, I'll take it.
Bakalım - Let's see.

Ne yapalım - What shall we do?

Anlamadınsa bir kez daha anlatayım - If you have not understood, let me explain it again.

Ne olursa olsun - Be it as it may.

The subjunctive past is formed by adding "-idi" to the base. It is rare as it is only used to express a hopeless wish. It can be introduced by "keşke".

Keşke bunu yapsaydık - Would that we had done that!

Atasözü - Proverb

Beygirin suratını değil, süratını överler.

They praise a horse for its speed, not its face

(Same meaning as the English proverb:
"Don't judge a book by its cover")

Chapter 11

Sundry Suffixes

11.1 - "ebil/abil" = to be able

The suffix "-ebil/-abil" ("-yebil/-yabil" after vowels) conveys the meaning of "being able to". The fact that this suffix happens to resemble the English word "able" is a useful aid. Note that this suffix does not fully operate according to vowel harmony.

> yapmak (to do) > yap-abil-mek (to be able to do)
> yap-abil-i-yorum - I can do (it)
> yap-abil-diniz - you were able to do (it).
> yap-abil-dik - we were able to (it).
> Bunu yap-abil-ecek misiniz? - Are you going to be able to do this?

You can add the "-ebil/-abil" suffix to verbal nouns.

> gid-ebil-enler - those able to go
> oku-yabil-diğim kitaplar - the books I was able to read

With the negative:

> yap-ma-y-abil-irim - I may not be able to do (it).
> Bunu yap-ma-y-abil-irim - I may not be able to do this.
> Gel-me-y-ebil-irim - I may be unable to come.

11.2 - "-dir/-dır/-tir/-tır", "-t/-it/-üt/-ıt/-ut", and "-ir/-ür/-ır/-ur" = The Causative Suffixes

Causative verbs are used when the verb action is done to someone or something else, or when someone or something else is forced to carry out the verb action. The direct object of a causative verb is in the definite objective case (i.e., gets a "-i/-ü/-ı/-u" ending) while the agent made to do the action is in the dative case (i.e., gets an "-e/-a" ending)

yemek (to eat) > ye-dir-mek (to feed)
ölmek (to die) > öl-dür-mek (to kill)
unutmak (to forget) > unut-tur-mak (to cause to forget)
yazmak (to write) > yaz-dır-mak (to make someone write)

If a vowel stem consists of two or more syllables add a "-t"

okumak (to read) > oku-t-mak (to teach, to educate)
anlamak (to understand) > anla-t-mak (to explain)
beklemek (to wait) > bekle-t-mek (to keep someone waiting)
oturmak (to sit) > otur-t-mak (to seat)

There are a few single syllable verb stems (most of which end in a "k") which also take the "-t" plus a vowel.

korkmak (to fear) > kork-ut-mak (to frighten, to scare)
akmak (to flow) > ak-ıt-mak (to let flow)
kesmek (to cut) > kes-tir-mek (to have cut) > kes-tir-t-mek (to have someone make someone else cut something)

There are a number of single syllable verb stems which add "-r" with the appropriate vowel to form the causative.

bitmek > bit-ir-mek (to finish, to bring to an end)
geçmek > geç-ir-mek (to spend [time])
batmak > bat-tır-mak (to cause to sink)
doymak (to be satisfied/to have had enough) > doy-ur-mak (to satisfy)
duymak (to feel, to hear) > duy-ur-mak (to announce)
düşmek (to fall) > düş-ür-mek (to cause to fall)
kaçmak (to escape) > kaç-ır-mak (to kidnap)
yatmak (to lie down) > yat-ır-mak (to put to bed)
çıkmak (to go up, to go out) > çık-ar-mak (to extract, to deduce)
gitmek (to go) > gid-er-mek (to remove)
kopmak (to break) > kop-ar-mak (to break off)

There are two irregular causatives:

kalkmak (to rise, to depart) > kal-dır-mak (to raise, to remove)
görmek (to see) > gös-ter-mek (to show)

Mektubu yazdırdım - I got the letter written.
Mektubu ona yazdırdım - I got him to write the letter.

11.3 - "-Meli/-malı" = should, ought

The suffix "-meli/-malı" is used to communicate the idea of "should" or "ought".

> İnsan her gün su iç-meli - People should drink water every day.
> Bir Müslüman içki içme-meli - A Muslim shouldn't drink alcohol.
> Bir işe başlamadan önce iyi düşün-meli-sin. - You ought to think carefuly before starting a job.
> Kanuna göre davran-malı-yız. - We ought to behave according to the law.
> Haberi onlara erken ver-meli-yiz. - We should give the news to them early.

There are several other words which translate as "must", "should", or "ought". These words can often be used interchangeably.

"lazım" (necessary), "gerek" (necessary), "gerekli" (necessity, i.e, as an adjective of "gerekmek" - to be necessary)

> Müdüre gitmeniz lazım/gerek/gerekli/gerekiyor - You have to go to the director.
> Sınavı geçmek isterseniz, bu kitapları okumanız lazım/gerekiyor. - If you want to pass the test you have to read these books.

"zor" (difficult, force, obligation, necessary)

> Ankara'ya gitmek zorundayım - I am obliged to go to Ankara
> Onunla görüşmek zorunda - He has to see him.

11.4 - More Endings

"-ip/ıp/üp/up" The suffix "-ip" is used in place of repeating pairs of verbs that have the same subject and are in the same tense. If the second verb is negative and the first verb is positive the first verb (the one ending in "-ip") is followed by "de".

> Gelebileceğim ve çay içebileceğim > gel-ip çay içebileceğim (I'll be able to come and I'll be able to drink tea).
> Elbiselerini yıkadı ve astı > Elbiselerini yika-y-ıp astı (He washed and hung up his clothes).
> Kalktı ve gitti > Kalk-ıp gitti (He got up and left).

Kalk-ıp da gitmedi - He got up but he didn't go.

To communicate the concept "I don't know whether he will or not" the verb stem is repeated, the first with "-ip".

Gid-ip gitmeyeceğini bilmiyor - He doesn't know whether he is leaving or not.

İşini zamanında bitir-ip bitiremeyeceğini bilmiyorum - I don't know whether or not he is going to be able to finish his work on time.

"-daş/taş" = "fellow", "togetherness" or "sameness". This suffix is not subject to vowel harmony.

arka-daş - friend (i.e. back fellow)
çağ-daş - contemporary (same age)
meslek-taş - colleague (someone having the same profession)
vatan-daş - citizen (same home-land)
yol-daş - comrade (on the same road)

"-esi/asi" = used in cursing

Kör ol-ası - may he become blind!
İpe gel-esi - may he come to the rope!

"-cik" indicates diminutives ("little," "dear little" or "poor little") and is often used with the first person ending. Nouns ending in a "k" may drop their "k" before this suffix.

anne-ciğ-im - my mummy
baba-cığ-ım - my daddy
ufak > ufa-cık - tiny

"-ce" = quite. This suffix may increase as well as diminish the force of the adjective or adverb to which it is attached.

iyi-ce - quite good
kötü-ce - quite bad

"-ceğiz, -cağız" = poor

adam-cağız - poor chap
kız-cağız - poor girl

"-(i)msi/-imtrak/-si" = like the English "-ish", "-si" is used when the modified noun or adjective ends in a consonant.

sarı-msı, sarı-mtrak - yellowish
beyaz-ımsı, beyaz-ımtrak - whitish
ekşi-msi, ekşi-mtrak – sourish
çocuk-su - childish
erkek-si - mannish, manly

"-(y)ici". Denotes an occupation or regular activity.

okumak > oku-y-ucu (reader)
dinlemek > dinle-y-ici (listener)
akmak (to flow) > ak-ıcı (flowing, fluent)
satmak (to sell) > satı-cı (salesperson)
güldürmek (to make laugh) > güldür-ücü (funny, amusing)

Atasözü

Gülü seven dikenine katlanır

He who loves roses must put up with thorns

Chapter 12

Indefinite Pronouns, Numbers, And So On.

12.1 - Indefinite Pronouns

Many indefinite pronouns are formed by the word "biri" (someone). It may follow a singular noun in the genitive.

> Biri şu yana gitti, biri bu yana - One went this way, one went that way.
> birisi - someone
> Birisi bana telefon etmeye çalışıyor - Someone is trying to telephone
>   me.
> Böyle birisi yok - There is no such person.
> Adamın biri - some man
> Herifin biri bize pencereden bakıyor - Some jerk is looking at us through
>   the window.
> öğrencilerden biri - one of the students
> işçilerden biri - one of the workers
>
> şey - thing
> Şeyi gördük - We saw what's his/her name.
> Şeyi nerede? - Where is what-do-you-call-it?

12.2 - Cardinal and Ordinal Numbers

Ordinal numbers are formed by adding the suffix "-inci" or "nci" (depending on whether the number ends in a vowel) to cardinal numbers. Vowel harmony is maintained.

> bir (one) > bir-inci (first)
> iki (two) > iki-nci (second)
> üç (three) > üçü-ncü (third)
> dört (four) > dörd-üncü (fourth)

beş (five) > beş-inci (fifth)
altı (six) > altı-ncı (sixth)
yedi (seven) > yedi-nci (seventh)
sekiz (eight) > sekiz-inci (eighth)
dokuz (nine) > dokuz-uncu (ninth)
on (ten) > on-uncu (tenth)
onbir (eleven) > onbir-inci (eleventh)
oniki (twelve) > oniki-nci (twelfth)
yirmi (twenty) > yirmi-nci (twentieth)
otuz (thirty) > otuz-uncu (thirtieth)
kırk (forty) > kırk-ıncı (fourtieth)
elli (fifty) > elli-nci (fiftieth)
altmış (sixty) > altmış-ıncı (sixtieth)
yetmiş (seventy) > yetmiş-inci (seventieth)
seksen (eigthy) > seksen-inci (eightieth)
doksan (ninety) > doksan-ıncı (ninetieth)
yüz (one hundred) > yüz-üncü (hundredth)
bin (one thousand) > bin-inci (thousandth)
milyon (one million) > milyon-uncu (millionth)

12.3 - Distributive numerals

Distributive numerals (i.e. "once each") are formed by adding the suffix "-şer" to those numbers which end in a vowel and "-er" to those which end in a consonant. Vowel harmony is maintained.

bir-er - one each
iki-şer - two each/by twos
üç-er - three each
altı-şar - six each
yarım-şar - half each
Çocuklara bir-er Fanta verdi - He gave the children one Fanta each.

Note: kaç (how many) > kaç-ar (how many each?)

12.3 - "So-and-so", "Such-and such", "And so on", "And all that", "Thereabouts", "So-manyeth"

"Falan", "filan", "filanca" (so-and-so, "such-and-such"). "Falan" and "filan" can also mean "and so on" or "and all that".

Filan günde Hopa'ya gitti - On such-and-such a day he went to Hopa.

Mektup falan geldi mi? - Have any letters (or cards or parcels) come?

Burada öğretmen falan yok - There is no teacher (or other supervisor) here.

Yazın falan gidecekmiş - He's supposed to go in the summer.

"Filance" (so-manyeth, number so-and-so)

Falanıncı odanın falanıncı rafında aradığın kitabı bulacaksın - You'll find the book in room number so-and-so on the so-manyeth shelf.

Another way of saying "and all that" is by repeating the word in question but submitting an "m" for the first consonant of the second word. (For words that begin with an "m" you have to use "falan").

Burada defter mefter yok - There's no notebook (or other writing paper) here.

Köyde okul mokul yok - There's no school (or anything like it) in the village.

Atasözü - Proverb

İş anlayanda değil, bitirende derler.

They say that he who finishes a job is more worthy than he who understands it.

Key Verbs

Case endings:
accusative case (i), genitive case (in), dative case (a),
locative case (da), ablative case (dan).

açmak (ı) - to open
almak (ı) - to take, receive, buy
anlamak (ı) - understand
aramak (ı) - to seek
atmak (ı) - to throw
bakmak (a) - to look
başlamak (ı) - to begin
beklemek (ı) - to wait, expect
bırakmak (ı) - to leave
bilmek (ı) - to know
bulmak (ı) - to find
çalışmak (a) - to work, try
çekmek (ı) - to pull, draw, to suffer
çıkmak (dan) - to go out, to go up
demek (a) - to say
dinlemek (ı) - to listen
doğmak - to be born
dolaşmak (ı) - to wander
durmak (ı) - to stand, to stop
duymak (ı) - to feel, to hear
düşmek - to fall
düşünmek (ı) - to think
etmek - to do
geçmek (dan) - to pass
gelmek (a) - to come
getirmek (ı, dan, a) - to bring
girmek (a) - to enter
gitmek (dan, a) - to go
göndermek (ı, a) - to send
görmek (ı, dan) - to see
göstermek (ı, a) - to show
hasta olmak - to be sick

hatırlamak (ı) - to remember
içmek (ı) - to drink
istemek (ı) - to want, to ask for
kaldırmak (ı) - to raise
kalkmak - to rise
kapamak (ı) - to shut
kapatmak (ı) - to close, to cover
kaybetmek (ı) - to lose
kazanmak (ı) - to win
kırmak (ı) - to break
konuşmak (ı, la) - to speak (to)
koşmak - to run
koymak (ı) - to put
kullanmak (ı) - to use
okumak (ı) - to read
olmak - to be, to become, to occur, to
mature
oturmak (a) - to sit, to dwell
öğrenmek (ı) - to learn
öğretmek (ı) - to teach
ölmek - to die
öpmek (ı) - to kiss
sanmak (ı) - to suppose
satmak (ı, a) - to sell
saymak (ı) - to count
seçmek (ı) - to choose
sevmek (ı) - to love
seyahat etmek (a) - to travel
sormak (ı) - to ask
söylemek (ı) - to tell
tanımak (ı) - to recognise, to know
tanışmak (la) - to be introduced

tanıştırmak (ı, la) - to introduce
taşımak (ı, dan, a) - to carry
tatbik etmek (ı) - to apply
telefon etmek (a) - to telephone
tutmak (ı) - to hold
uçmak - to fly
unutmak (ı) - to forget
uyanmak - to awake
uyumak - to sleep
vermek (ı, a) - to give

vurmak (ı, a)- to strike, to hit
yapmak (ı) - to make, to do
yardım etmek (a) - to help
yaşamak (da, ı) - to live
yatmak (a, da) - to lie down
yazmak (ı) - to write
yemek (ı) - to eat
yürümek - to walk
yüzmek - to swim

Index of Suffixes

-ma/-me - 4.7
-madan/-meden - 6.5
-mak/-mek - 2.3; 6.7; 9.8
-maksızın/-meksizin - 6.5
-maktansa/-mektense - 6.5
-malı/-meli - 11.3
-me/-ma - 4.7; 9.8; 9.9
-me/-ma/-mı/-mi/-mu-/mü - 4.7; 4.8; 4.9
-mez/-maz - 4.10; 4.11
-mı/-mi/-mu/-mü - 8.5
-mış/-miş - 10.1; 10.2
-n - 1.5; 10.6; 10.7
-niz – 1.5
-r - 4.3; 4.4
-sa/-se -5.1;5.2;5.3
-sana - 5.7
-sanıza - 5.7
-sel - 7.4
-sene - 5.7
-senize - 5.7
-sı/-si - 1.5; 1.6; 6.3; 11.4
-sın/-sin - 2.1; 2.2
-sın/-sin/-sun/-sün - 8.6; 10.9
-sınız/-siniz - 2.1; 2.2

-sız/-siz - 5.10
-sun - 2.7
-sunuz - 2.1; 2.7
-ş - 10.8
-şar/-şer - 12.3
-t/-ıt/-it/-ut/-üt - 11.2
-ta/-te - 3.6
-tan/-ten - 3.7
-tı/-ti - 2.4; 4.2
-tık/-tik- 2.4; 4.2
-tım/-tim - 2.4; 4.2
-tım/-tin - 2.4; 4.2
-tınız/-tiniz - 2.4; 4.2
-tılar/-tiler - 2.4; 4.2
-tür-2.1
-u/-ü - 3.3
-u/-ü/-ı/-i - 7.5
-uk/-ük/-ık/-ik - 7.5
-um/-üm/-ım/-im - 1.2; 1.5; 2.7; 7.5
-un/-ün - 3.4
-untu/-üntü/-ıntı/-inti - 7.5
-uz - 2.1; 2.7
-üz - 2.1
-ya - 6.3
-yor - 2.6; 2.7

54254568R00048

Made in the USA
Columbia, SC
27 March 2019